Yoshiko Tsukiori

sewing for your girls

Easy Instructions for Dresses, Smocks and Frocks

TUTTLE Publishing

Tokyo | Rutland, Vermont | Singapore

contents

basics of dressmaking

page 5   Basic Procedures for Sewing Clothes
     Sizing
6   Sewing Equipment
     About Needles and Thread
7   Fabrics Used in This Book
     About Fabric
8   How to Transfer Patterns
9   Cutting Out Fabric
10   How to Mark Symbols
12   How to Use a Sewing Machine

step by step

page 14   How to Make
15   1. Create and Attach Pocket
17   2. Create Slash Opening
18   3. Sew Shoulders
     4. Create Bias Tape
19   5. Bind Neckline Using Bias Tape
     6. Create Shoulder Frill

page 20   7. Attach Shoulder Frill, Finish Off Armholes Using Bias Tape
21   8. Sew Sides
     9. Sew Armholes
22   10. Fold Up Hem Twice and Sew

page 4
basic pattern
[how to make basic pattern #1]

page 23
applied pattern
[Applied Pattern #1 a,b]

page 24
basic pattern
[how to make basic pattern #2]

page 25
applied pattern
[Applied Pattern #2 a,b]

page 26
basic pattern
[how to make basic pattern #3]

page 27
applied pattern
[Applied Pattern #3]

page 28
basic pattern
[how to make basic pattern #4]

page 29
applied pattern
[Applied Pattern #4]

basic sewing techniques

page 37 Basic Techniques for Sewing Girls' Clothes
38 Making a Knot/Handy Tool: Threader
39 How to Sew on a Button
40 Double-folded Edging/
Narrow Double-folded Edging
41 Single-folded Edging/Blind Hem Stitch
42 How to Create a Back Opening/
How to Create a Loop from Fabric
43 How to Attach Tape/Using Tulle
44 How to Attach a Frill
45 Attaching a Frill from Above (1) (2)
46 Finishing Off a Neck Opening with a
Facing

page 47 Attaching a Collar (1)
48 Attaching a Collar (2)
49 Attaching a Collar (3)
52 Attaching a Sleeve
56 Finishing Off an Armhole
with a Facing
58 How to Sew Pants
59 How to Sew Shirring
Elastic
60 How to Sew Overalls

page 62 How to Insert an Invisible Zipper
63 Handy Tool: Zipper Foot
64 How to Attach a Hook and Eye
65 How to Sew a Smock
66 How to Sew a Partial Opening
68 How to Do Smocking
(for Gingham Check)
70 How to Do Smocking
(for Plain Fabric)
How to Make a Pocket
71 Instructions for All Garments

page 30
basic pattern
[how to make basic pattern #5]

page 31
applied pattern
[Applied Pattern #5]

page 32
basic pattern
[how to make basic pattern #6]

page 33
applied pattern
[Applied Pattern #6 a,b]

page 34
basic pattern
[how to make basic pattern #7]

page 35
applied pattern
[Applied Pattern #7]

page 36
basic pattern
[how to make basic pattern #8]

AUTHOR'S NOTE
In order to make it easier for readers to imagine their own designs and be able to create clothes in fabrics other than those in this book, I've made garments in plain fabric versions in addition to the printed ones. There are easy-to-follow instructions alongside the photos, so even beginner sewers can make the clothes. I hope you enjoy experimenting with the designs using your favorite fabrics.

[Basic Pattern #1]

basic pattern

basics of dressmaking→p.5～

step by step→p.14～

Basic Procedures for Sewing Clothes

Broadly speaking, there are about seven steps involved in making clothes.

Once you've decided which garments to make from this book, follow these steps:

1 ♣	Decide on the design
2 ♣	Check the amount of fabric required
3 ♣	Gather fabric and other notions together
4 ♣	Prepare fabric
5 ♣	Transfer pattern
6 ♣	Cut out fabric
7 ♣	Sew

 ## Sizing

Measurements are given in both inches and metrics. Metric measurements are more precise, and using them can result in a better cut, drape and fit. All inch measurements are approximate, but effort has been made to convert materials measurements to standard US fabric and tape/ribbon widths, yardage and zipper lengths. Children's measurements and pattern drafting conversions are as comparable as possible to actual metric measurements.

- The garments in this book are based on the size chart below, so are suitable for children of heights 39½, 43½, 47¼, 51¼, 55 in (100, 110, 120, 130, 140cm).
- Measure your child and select the pattern to suit.
- Adjust the lengths of blouses, dresses, pants and so on to suit your child. Many designs are comfortably loose and can be worn for 1–2 years, depending on how fast the child grows. For example, the blouse below is for a child 39½ in (100cm) tall, so balance-wise it looks different—but still cute—on the models wearing it, who are 37½ (95cm) and 41½ (105cm) tall.

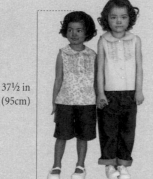

37½ in (95cm)

41½ in (105cm)

Size reference chart—in (cm)

Height	39½ (100)	43½ (110)	47¼ (120)	51¼ (130)	55 (140)
Bust	21¼ (54)	23 (58)	24½ (62)	26 (66)	28 (70)
Waist	19½ (49)	20 (51)	21 (53)	22 (55)	22½ (57)
Hip	22½ (57)	24 (61)	25½ (65)	27½ (70)	29½ (75)

Sewing Equipment

The tools on this page are for making patterns, cutting fabric, marking symbols and sewing.
They make the sewing process smooth and enjoyable.

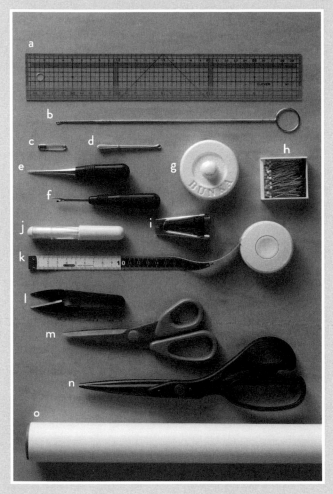

a GRAPH RULER—a transparent graph ruler is useful for drafting seam allowance lines, and because it's pliable it makes measuring armholes and curved lines easy (→p.8)

b LOOP TURNER—for creating fabric loops (→p.42)

c SAFETY PINS—use to attach to the end of elastic to make it easier to pass through narrow casings (→p.47, 53, 58)

d THREADER—grips the end of thread or elastic to make threading easier

e AWL—use to turn out corners, mark symbols, remove stitches or when sewing gathers (→p.44)

f UNPICKER—also called a seam ripper or hole cutter, for making buttonholes, also used for removing stitches

g WEIGHT—use to keep paper in place when transferring pattern pieces or hold fabric steady when cutting (→p.8)

h DRESSMAKING PINS—use when cutting fabric and sewing (→p.9)

i TAPE MAKER—use to make your own bias binding/tape from fabric. In this book, 12mm and 18mm (app. ½ in and ¾ in) widths are used (→p.18)

j DRESSMAKER'S CHALK PEN—this pen type is useful for marking fine lines and symbols on fabric (→p.9, 45)

k TAPE MEASURE—use to measure your child's size and lengths of fabric

l THREAD SNIPPERS—for trimming thread and cutting tricky areas

m PAPER SCISSORS—for cutting out patterns (→p.8)

n FABRIC SCISSORS—for cutting out fabric pattern pieces, making notches in fabric and so on (→p.9)

o TRACING PAPER—use transparent lined paper for transferring patterns. The roll type has no fold lines so is easy to use (→p.8)

 ## About Needles and Thread

Choose the right needle and thread for the fabric to ensure smooth sewing. Match the thread color to the fabric.

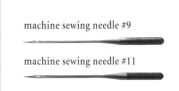 machine sewing needle #9

machine sewing needle #11

 Schappe Spun #90   Schappe Spun #60   Schappe Spun #30

 Resilon Thread   Tetron Thread

#9 machine sewing needle is used for light fabrics, while a #11 is used for most fabrics from cotton to linen.

For light fabrics use #90 (left). Most other fabrics like cotton and linen, can be sewn using #60 (center). Use #90 thread with #9 needle and #60 thread with #11 needle. Use #30 (right) when you want stitches to stand out or for sewing running stitch.

Resilon thread (left) has some elasticity to it so is used for sewing jersey and other knit fabrics. Tetron thread (right) is a multi-purpose.

Fabrics Used in This Book

The names and characteristics of the fabrics used in this book are listed here.

Cotton linen print

Cotton linen fabric with cute print of small flowers.

Double gauze

Two layers of gauze have been woven together to form this fabric which gets softer to the touch with every wash.

Cotton lawn

A lightweight, glossy plain weave fabric which is easy to cut and sew. It originated from linen made in Laon, France.

Linen chambray

There's a sporty air to this fabric, which is woven using colored warp threads and white weft threads.

Printed cotton

Lightweight cotton printed with a floral pattern. Take care when cutting fabric if you have chosen a large pattern.

Embroidered cotton

A design is machine-embroidered onto the fabric and finished off on the reverse side.

Sweatshirt fabric

Knit fabric with plain stitch on the outer side and pile on the inner side. Sew with stretch thread to avoid mistakes.

Liberty print

Cotton lawn by Liberty of London, known for its floral print in a multitude of colors.

Gingham check

Fabric woven using white and colored threads to create a check pattern.

 ## About Fabric

Fabric has a tendency to shrink when wet, so it should be rinsed to prepare it for use when sewing.

Number of times rinsed

once   twice   five times

When rinsing, the fabric should be completely wet before being dried. This ensures that garments made from the fabric won't shrink after washing. Fabric that has not been rinsed may still have coating on it that makes it stiff (left). Rinsing it once will soften it slightly (center). After being rinsed five times the fabric is quite soft (right).

Creases

If fabric such as cotton lawn has folding creases in it after being rinsed, iron it before cutting out pattern pieces.

Patterns and prints

For floral patterns and other designs that have a distinct top and bottom, make sure you cut all pattern pieces to face the right way.

How to Transfer Patterns

When you have decided what to make, transfer the full-size pattern to your own paper.

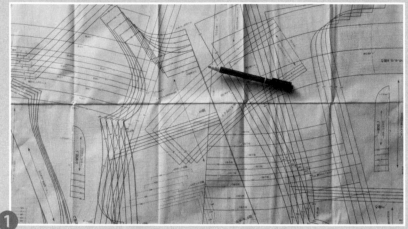

1 Once you have worked out which pieces you need and taken your child's measurements, use a marker to define pattern pieces so you won't make a mistake.

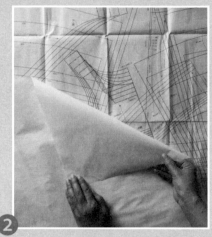

2 Lay tracing paper over the full-size pattern.

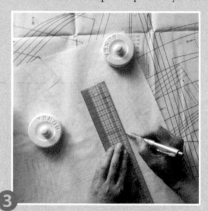

3 Use a graph ruler and pencil to transfer the center line. A weight prevents the tracing paper from slipping.

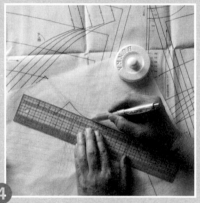

4 Move the graph ruler bit by bit to trace curves such as along the neck opening.

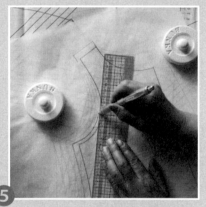

5 Once you have traced over the entire pattern, refer to the cutting layout and add seam allowances where necessary. A graph ruler is useful for this because it allows. you to draft parallel lines.

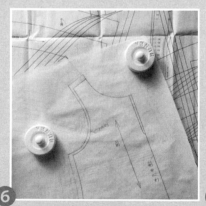

6 When seam allowances have been added, mark in the name of the pattern pieces, the grain line and other matching symbols.

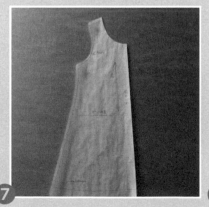

7 Cut out along seam allowance lines.

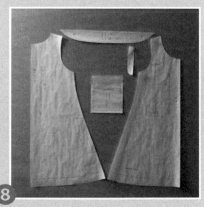

8 Transfer all parts and cut out.

Cutting Out Fabric

Fold the fabric as per the cutting layout and place pattern pieces on fabric to cut out. This method allows for cutting out without wasting fabric, but if the fabric has a one-way print, make sure to allow for this when cutting.

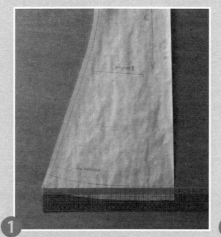

1 Measure across the widest part of the pattern—in this case, the width at the hemline.

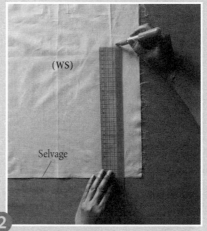

2 Mark the length of step 1 from the selvage using dressmaker's chalk.

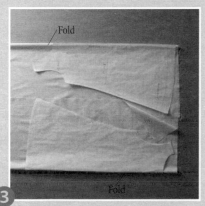

3 Fold fabric so the fold is parallel to the selvage. Place the center line of the pattern along the fold of the fabric and pin in place (fold the hem of the fabric out of the way).

3' Place pattern pieces on fabric folded in from both sides to eliminate waste.

4 Measure the length of bias tape needed by placing the graph ruler at the start of where the bias tape will be attached (armholes or neck openings) and curving the ruler around.

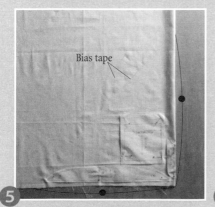

5 Change the fold of the fabric and position the remaining pattern pieces to be cut. Use dressmaker's chalk to draft the bias tape.

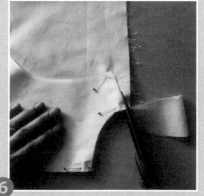

6 Hold fabric in place while cutting around pattern pieces.

7 All the pattern pieces cut out.

How to Mark Symbols

Cut a triangle to mark the center line, clip about ⅛ in (0.3cm) to mark where to place the end of a frill or indicate the shoulder line, and use an awl to make holes to show pocket positioning.

Match symbols and pin pieces together, then sew according to the indicated seam allowance using the scale on the sewing machine feed plate.

Mark the center front

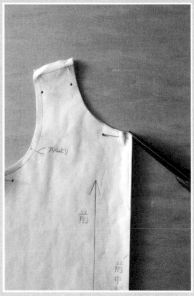

Clip a triangle of about ⅛ in (0.3cm) into the center front neckline.

Open out…

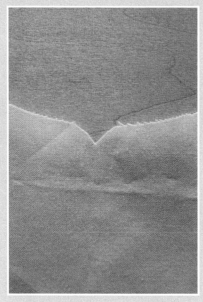

The notch created from cutting a triangle.

Mark the end of an opening

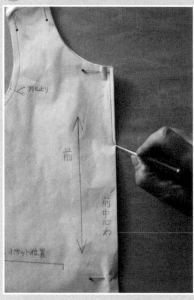

Make a hole at the very edge of the fold to mark the end of an opening.

Mark the position of a pocket

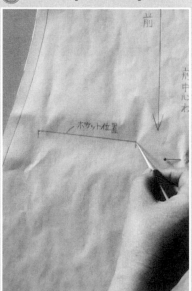

Make holes with an awl to mark the position of a pocket.

Remove the pattern piece…

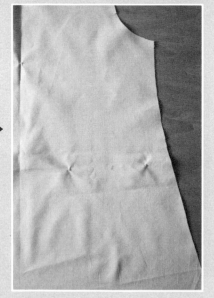

Symbols for pocket position made on garment front.

Enlarged image

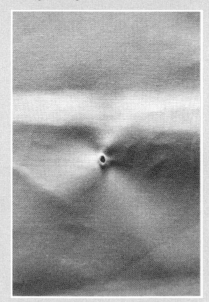

Hole made to indicate pocket position. Be careful not to cut fabric when making hole.

⦿ Mark position of the end of a frill

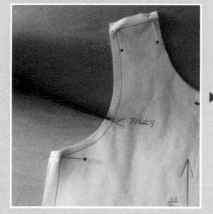

Clip at mark to indicate where frill ends.

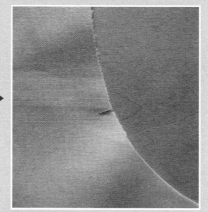

Clip in fabric showing where frill ends.

⦿ Mark a shoulder or hem line

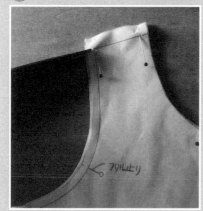

Clip at shoulder line (on armhole side).

Clip side to indicate hem.

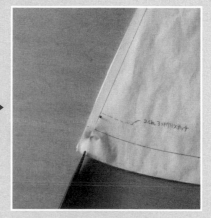

Clip edge of hem in the same way.

⦿ Mark finished lines of pocket

Clip into edge of pocket.

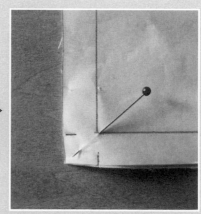

Clip into other corners.

How to Use a Sewing Machine

When the necessary symbols have been marked on the pattern pieces they are ready to be sewn.

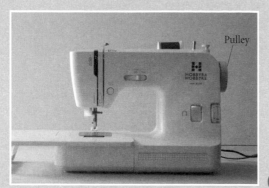

Pulley

Threading the machine

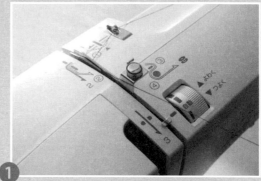

1 Thread as per the instructions supplied with the sewing machine. This is the upper thread.

2 Pass the upper thread through the needle, then hold the thread while turning the hand wheel (the round part on the top right of the machine) towards you to lower the needle. Keep turning until the needle has picked up the bobbin thread.

3 Take both upper and lower threads to the back of the machine.

Start sewing

 ▶

Match the edge of the fabric to the feed plate depending on the width of the seam allowance (image shown is for ⅜ in (1cm) seam allowance). Insert the needle.

Sew ¼–⅜ in (0.5cm–1cm) of stitches in reverse to lock the stitching before proceeding.

Finish sewing

Sew a few stitches in reverse as per the start of the seam. Clip threads close to start of stitching.

⚙ Making a plain seam

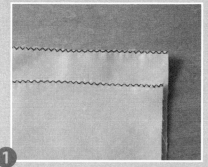

1 Neaten both raw edges using a zigzag stitch on the sewing machine.

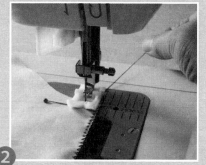

2 Match right sides of fabric and pin together. To make sure the fabric doesn't get caught up, gently pull the two threads (this is important) while starting to sew (→p.12 starting to sew).

3 Pull the fabric gently between both hands to progress with sewing.

4 Iron fabric from wrong side to even out any raised stitches. This is an important step in achieving a neat result.

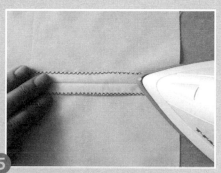

5 Use the flat of your fingers to open out the seam while pressing flat with an iron.

⚙ Making a seam that folds to one side

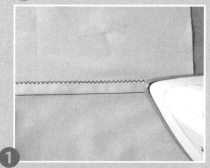

1 Complete steps 2–3 as above, then finish off seam by sewing with a zigzag stitch. Fold seam to one side and press.

2 On outer side, spread fabric on either side of seam while ironing to flatten it out.

Example of badly done seam

If steps 1–2 are not completed properly, fabric will crease incorrectly, so take care with these steps.

This A-line dress has sweet frills on the shoulders. It is easily slipped on over the head and has ties at the front neck opening. It can be worn by itself, or with jeans or leggings.

[how to make] basic pattern #1

basic pattern

page 4
See full-size pattern, side A

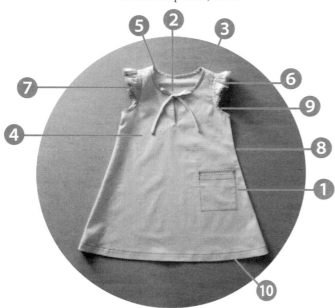

Cutting layout

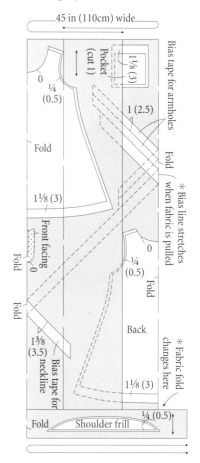

* For heights 47½–55 in [120-140cm]
(for heights 39½–47½ inches [100, 110,
120cm] see p. 9 step 3)

* Seam allowances are ⅜ in (1cm)
unless otherwise indicated

* Shaded area indicates fusible
interfacing

MATERIALS

【Unless sizes are specified, material amounts given are for all sizes】

FABRIC

Cotton linen print 45 in (110cm) wide

for child 39½ in (100cm) tall: 1⅓ yd (1m 20cm);

for 43½ in (110cm) tall: 1½ yd (1m 40cm); for 47¼ in (120cm) tall:
2 yd (1m 80cm); for 51¼ in (130cm) tall: 2⅛ yd (1m 90cm);

for 55 in (140cm) tall: 2⅛ yd (2m)

Fusible interfacing 4x6 in (10×15cm)

Fusible double-sided tape ½–⅝ in (12mm)

Lace ½ in (1.3cm) wide:

for child 39½, 43½, 47¼ in (100, 110, 120cm) tall: 1⅛ yd (1m);

for child 51¼ in (130cm) tall:1¼ yd (1m 10cm);

for child 55 in (140cm) tall—1⅓ yd (1m 20cm)

* Length of bias tape required for armhole is the measurement of the
completed armhole plus seam allowance (create 2)

* Length of bias tape required for neckline is the measurement of the completed
neckline + length of tie 10¾ in(27cm) x2 + length of fold at ends (2)

INSTRUCTIONS (→p.15~22)

Preparation: Apply fusible interfacing
to front facing. *M stitch around outer
edge

1 Create pocket and attach to front

2 Create front opening.

3 Sew shoulders. M stitch through
both layers

4 Create bias tape

5 Bind neckline using bias tape

6 Create shoulder frill.

7 Attach shoulder frill, bind armholes
using bias tape

8 Sew sides. M stitch through both layers

9 Finish off armholes

10 Fold hem up twice and sew

* M = use a zigzag stitch to neaten seam
allowance

Create and Attach Pocket

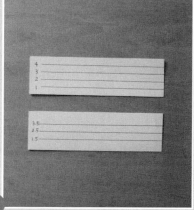

1 Create a ruler for the iron. Rule parallel lines ⅜ in (1cm) apart on card about 8 x 2 in (20 x 5cm) and about the same thickness as a postcard.

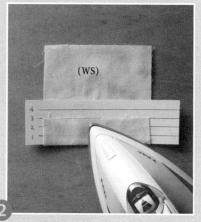

2 Fold pocket opening over twice. For a ⅞ in (2cm) fold, match up the clip marking (→p.11) with the 1⅛ in (3cm) mark on the ironing ruler and fold.

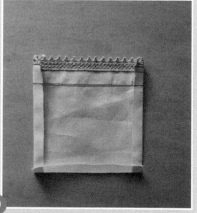

3 Keeping the pocket in the same position, fold the edge under along the ⅞ in (2cm) mark on the ironing ruler.

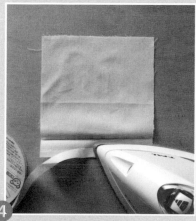

4 Open out **3** and apply heat-fusible double-sided tape to seam allowance.

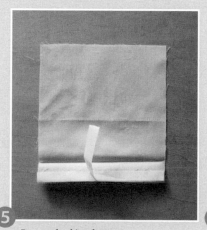

5 Remove backing from tape.

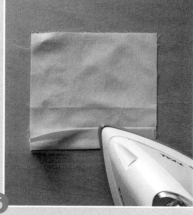

6 Fold at ⅞ in (2cm) width again and press. This step replaces basting.

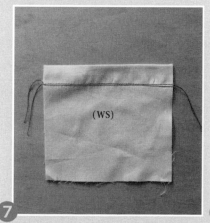

7 Sew about 1/16 in (0.1cm) from fold edge.

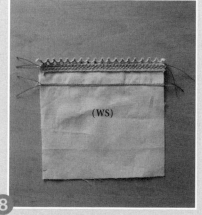

8 Stitch lace to pocket edge.

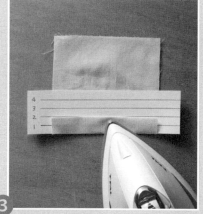

9 Fold three sides in towards center, using clip marks as a guide.

(continued from p15)

 Create pocket and attach to front

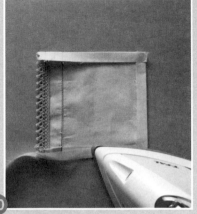

10 Apply heat fusible double sided tape to three sides and iron.

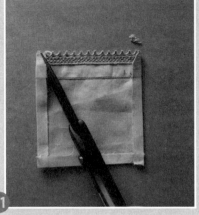

11 Trim seam allowances of pocket opening on the diagonal.

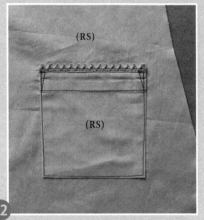

(RS)

(RS)

12 Match up pocket with markings on front, remove double sided tape backing and press into place. Stitch around pocket about 1/16 in (0.1cm) from edge.

 1-2

How to Reinforce Pocket Edges with Triangle Stitching

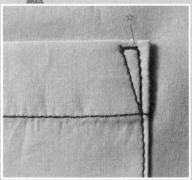

Pockets take a lot of wear and tear with hands going in and out so often. Reinforce the corners with two layers of stitching in a triangular shape.

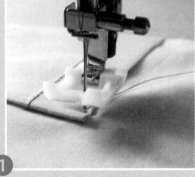

1 Insert needle about 1/4 in (0.5cm) from edge of pocket opening (marked with a star symbol) and sew towards edge.

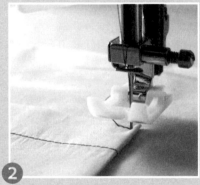

2 Leave needle in fabric at edge. Raise presser foot and reposition fabric to face downwards. Sew down along pocket edge.

3 At the point where the pocket opening fold adjoins the fabric, insert the needle and leave it in while repositioning the fabric.

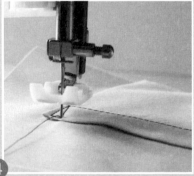

4 Sew until the star symbol. Sew over the top of the stitches from steps 1–3.

5 Sew around all three sides. Complete the other side of the pocket opening in the same way.

♣ 2 Create Slash Opening

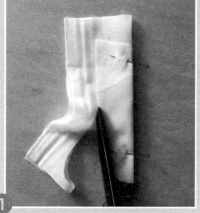

1 Use facing piece as a template to cut out fusible interfacing (do not add seam allowance).

2 Apply fusible interfacing to back of fabric, using a cloth over the top of the fabric when ironing.

3 Sew around the edge using a zigzag stitch. Use a pencil on the back of the fabric (the interfacing) to mark opening.

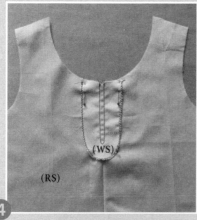

4 Match right sides of facing and dress front along center front. Sew along markings for opening.

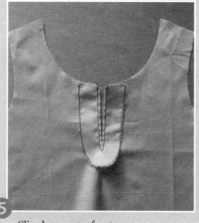

5 Clip along center front.

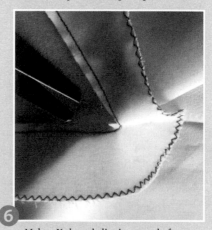

6 Make a Y shaped clipping at end of opening. Clip as close to stitching line as possible without cutting it.

7 Open out seams and press.

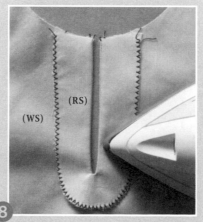

8 Turn facing to inside of dress and press.

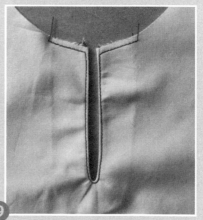

9 Stitch on right side of fabric 1/16 in (0.1cm) from edge. Stitch along neckline 1/4 in (0.5cm) from edge.

3 Sew Shoulders

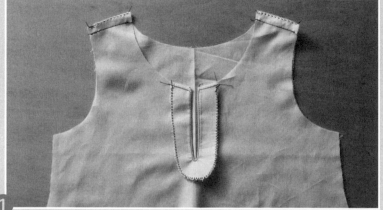

1 Place right sides of dress front and back together to match shoulders. Finish seams with a zigzag stitch.

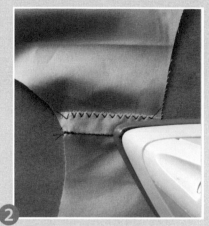

2 Press seam towards back.

4 Create Bias Tape

1 Insert strip of fabric to become bias tape into tape maker (tape maker shown is ¾ in [1.8cm] wide).

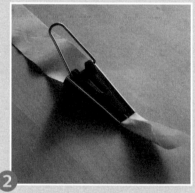

2 Pull fabric through end of tape maker. Both sides of fabric will be folded into the center.

3 Iron fabric as it comes out of tape maker to form bias tape.

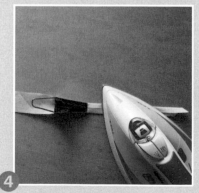

4 Top: Bias tape ¾ in (1.8cm) wide for neckline.
Bottom: Bias tape ½ in (1.2cm) wide for armholes.

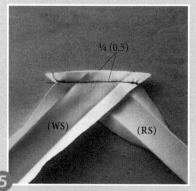

5 To join pieces of tape, open out folds and match right sides of fabric on the bias. Sew ¼ in (0.5cm) from edge.

¼ (0.5)

(WS) (RS)

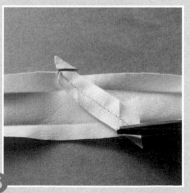

6 Open out seam and trim excess.

5 ♣ Bind Neckline Using Bias Tape

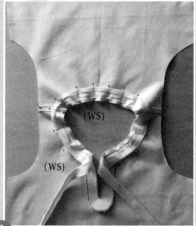

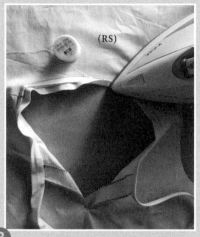

1 Place bias tape wrong side up around neckline of wrong side of dress and pin in place (match join of bias tape to left shoulder seam). Leave 10¾ in (27cm) of bias tape on each side to form ties.

2 Sew over bias tape fold line.

3 Turn right side out and iron binding along stitching line. As an alternative to basting, sandwich heat fusible thread between facing and neckline to keep binding in place.

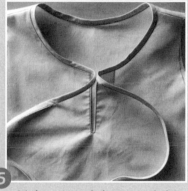

4 Fold over ⅜ in (1cm) at end of ties. To achieve a neat result, press the ends in at the center so they are sandwiched between the sides of the tape.

5 Stitch continuously from one end of tie to the other along the neckline.

6 ♣ Create Shoulder Frill

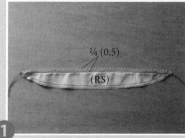

1 With right sides together, stitch lace to straight side of frill. Neaten edges using a zigzag stitch.

2 Press seam towards wrong side of fabric. On right side of fabric, sew 1/16 in (0.1cm) from edge to keep lace in position.

3 On curved side of frill, make two rows of gathering stitches (⅛ in and ⅜ in [0.3cm and 0.8cm] from fabric edge). Stitches should be ⅛ in (0.3–0.4cm) in length.

1 Match right sides of dress front and shoulder frill at shoulders and marks for end of frills. Pin in place.

2 Pull up gathering threads so frill lies flat against armhole.

3 Baste frill in place, sewing ⅛ in (0.3cm) from edge.

4 Position bias tape for armhole over the top of 3 and pin in place.

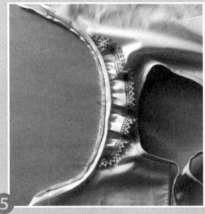

5 Sew along bias tape fold line.

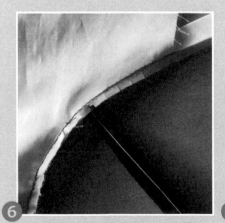

6 Clip into curve seam allowance at small intervals.

7 Turn right side out and press, using heat fusible thread to keep in place but leaving a few centimeters free at underarm. Trim end of bias tape in line with side.

8 ♣ Sew Sides

1 Open out bias tape at underarm and sew side in a continuous seam.

2 Neaten seam using a zigzag stitch.

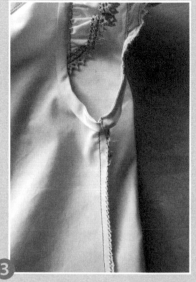

3 Press seam towards back. Fold bias tape as per previously and pin in place.

9 ♣ Sew Armholes

1 Sew around armholes.

2 Use an awl or unpicker to remove any gathering stitches showing on outer side of frill.

10 Fold Up Hem Twice and Sew

How to sew a double-folded curved hem

Fold up ⅞ in (2cm) of hem twice and sew.

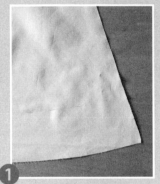

1 Use dressmaker's chalk to mark 2¼ in (6cm) (1⅛ in [3cm] seam allowance for hem x 2) from edge.

2 Bring edge of fabric to meet marks made in 1 and iron.

3 Use ironing ruler to fold edge down/in to form ⅞ in (2cm) hem.

[Basic Pattern #1]

basic pattern

page 4

Completed Dress

[Applied Pattern #1]

applied
pattern

techniques for creating details→p.42, 44(a), 45(b)
how to make it→p.71–72(a), 73(b)

[Basic Pattern #2]
basic pattern

techniques for creating details→p.46

how to make it→p.74

[Applied Pattern #2]

applied
pattern

techniques for creating details→p.47(a), 48(b), 52(a), 53(b)

how to make it→p.75(a), 76(b)

[Basic Pattern #3]

basic
pattern

techniques for creating details→p.54, 62–64, 68–70

how to make it→p.77

[Applied Pattern #3]

applied pattern

techniques for creating details→p.43, 62–64, 70

how to make it→p.78

[Basic Pattern #4]
basic pattern

techniques for creating details→p.58

how to make it→p.79

[Applied Pattern #4]

applied
pattern

techniques for creating details→p.60, 61

how to make it→p.80–81

[Basic Pattern #5]
basic pattern

techniques for creating details→p.59

how to make it→p.82

 [Applied Pattern #5]

applied
pattern

techniques for creating details→p.45, 59

how to make it→p.83–84

[Basic Pattern #6]

basic
pattern

techniques for creating details→p.65

how to make it→p.85–86

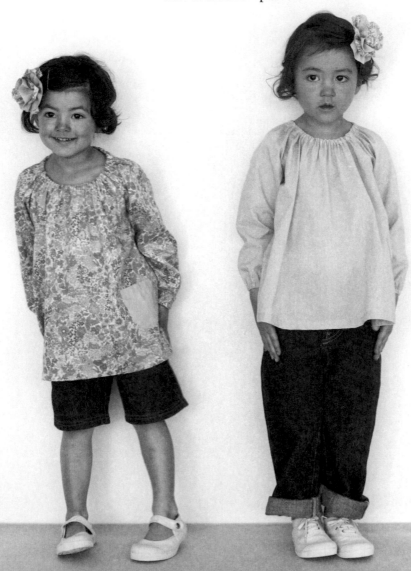

applied pattern

techniques for creating details→p.43(b)

how to make it→p.87(a), 88–89(b)

a

b

basic pattern

techniques for creating details→p.49–51, 56, 57

how to make it→p.90–91

[Applied Pattern #7]

applied
pattern

techniques for creating details→p.56, 57, 66, 67

how to make it→p.92

[Basic Pattern #8]

basic
pattern

techniques for creating details→p.42

how to make it→p.93–94

basic sewing techniques

Basic Techniques for Sewing Girls' Clothes

Basic sewing instructions for versions a and b of garments 1-8

Basic Techniques for Sewing Girls' Clothes

Don't worry if you're a beginner when it comes to sewing.
Have fun creating girls' clothes and use basic techniques to give them a neat finish
using the easy-to-follow advice shown here.

 ## Making a Knot

For blind hem stitch or when sewing on a button, use about 12–16 in (30–40cm) of thread and make a knot at the end.

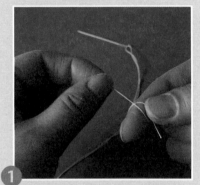 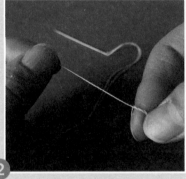 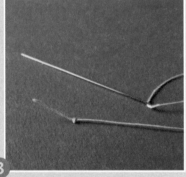

1 Pass the thread through the needle and wind the end around your finger once, holding it in place with your thumb.

2 Twist thread so it winds around on itself.

3 Pull thread tightly to form knot and cut excess thread to $1/16$ in (1–2mm).

Handy Tool #1

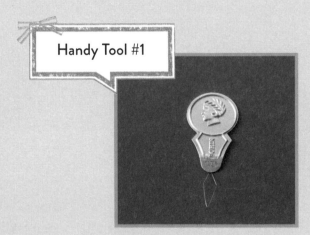

Threader
Pass thread through the loop, then insert the loop into the eye of a needle and pull thread through the eye.

How to Sew on a Button

When sewing on a button, use thick hand sewing thread (30-50).
If you don't have any, double a strand of machine sewing thread and use that instead.

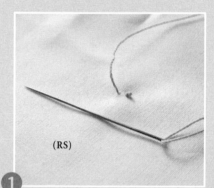

1 Make a knot in thread. On right side of material, insert needle and bring back out very close to entry point.

(RS)

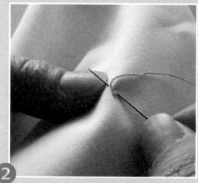

2 Sew back over this point.

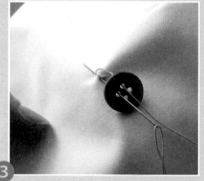

3 Insert needle into hole in button and bring back through other hole to secure to point 2.

4 Create a small gap by wedging your index finger under the button (to form the shank of the button) and pass the needle through the two holes 2–3 times. Repeat for other holes.

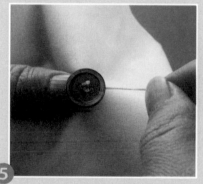

5 With your index finger still wedged under the button, wind thread around stitching at underside of button 3–4 times (this is the shank).

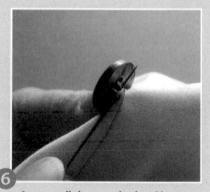

6 Insert needle between shank and button.

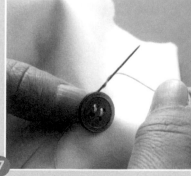

7 Hold needle with index finger and wind thread around it 2–3 times. Pull needle through to form a knot.

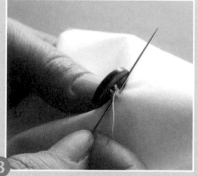

8 Pass needle back under shank and trim thread close to button.

9 If the shank height is the same as the thickness of the material, the garment will sit neatly when the button is done up.

39

Double-folded Edging

In this example, the edging is double-folded to a ⅞ in (2cm) width. Other widths are made the same way.

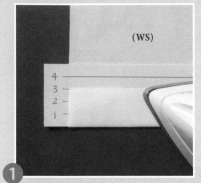

(WS)

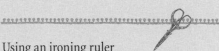

Using an ironing ruler

An ironing ruler can be made from thick card (about the same weight as a postcard) cut to about 8 x 2 in (20 x 5cm). Make parallel lines at ⅜ in (1cm) intervals (see p15). It's also helpful to make a second ruler marked at ⅝ in (1.5cm) intervals.

1 Use an ironing ruler to press edge of material up to 1⅛ in (3cm) mark.

2 Leave the ironing ruler in position and fold under ⅜ in (1cm) of material so edge is at the ⅞ in (2cm) mark.

3 Use heat-fusible double-sided tape in folded seam allowance in place of basting (if you don't have any tape, pin in place).

4 Sew to body of fabric ¹/₁₆ in (0.1cm) from folded edge.

 ## Narrow Double-folded Edging

This method creates a ⅜ in (1cm) edging. Even narrower edgings can be made in the same way.

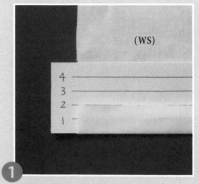

(WS)

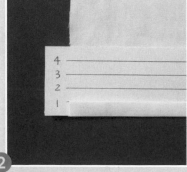

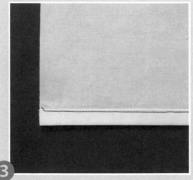

1 Use an ironing ruler to press edge of material up to the ⅞ in (2cm) mark.

2 Leave the ironing ruler in position and fold under ⅜ in (1cm) of material so edge is at the ⅜ in (1cm) mark.

3 Sew to body of fabric ¹/₁₆ in (0.1cm) from folded edge.

Single-folded Edging

In this example, the edging is single-folded to a 1 in (2.5cm) width. Other widths are made the same way.

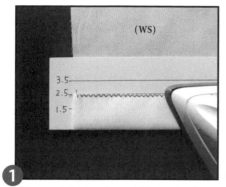

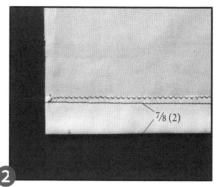

1 Zigzag stitch edge of material. Use an ironing ruler to press edge of material up to 1 in (2.5cm) mark.

2 Sew to body of fabric ¼ in (0.5cm) from edge.

 ## Blind Hem Stitch

This stitch is used for taking up hems on lightweight fabrics, but in this book, it is used to attach facings to seam allowances.

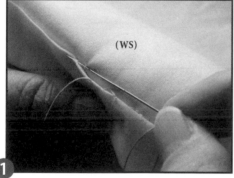

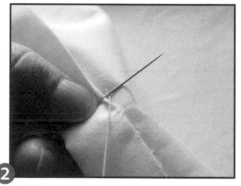

1 Bring needle out from seam allowance and pick up a thread in the fabric so no mark will be seen on the right side of the fabric. Insert the needle back into the seam allowance about ⅜ in (0.8cm) away on a diagonal angle, picking up about ⅛ in (0.2cm) of fabric.

2 When you have finished stitching, wind thread around needle 2–3 times.

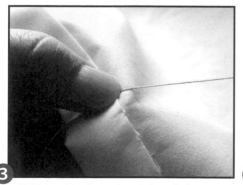

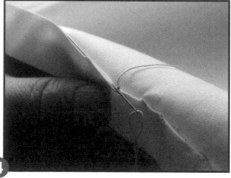

3 Hold thread in place to keep it from slackening and pull to form a knot.

4 Pass needle back into seam allowance for about ⅜ in (1cm), then trim thread close to fabric.

How to Create a Back Opening applied pattern 1a, 1b → p.23

This opening makes use of the existing seam. It's created by simply leaving part of the seam open.

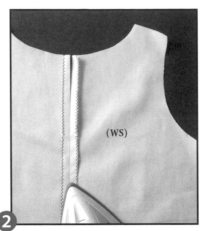

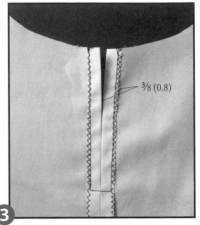

1 Sew edges of both pieces of fabric using zigzag stitch. With right sides of fabric facing, sew to endpoint of opening.

2 Press seam open.

3 Stitch along edges of fabric and across seam to keep opening in place.

Endpoint of opening

Back (WS)

(WS)

⅜ (0.8)

How to Create a Loop from Fabric applied pattern 1a, 1b → p.23   basic pattern 8 → p.36

Create a long strip of fabric and cut it to the desired length for a neat result.

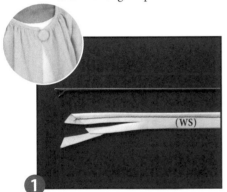

1 Fold bias tape so right sides match and stitch a ⅛ in (0.3cm) seam. Trim seam allowance to about ⅛ in (0.2cm). The loop turner is shown above.

2 Insert the loop turner into the tube created in step 1 and catch the end of the fabric in the hook.

3 Slowly pull the loop turner to turn the fabric right side out.

(WS)

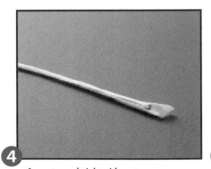

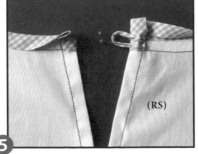

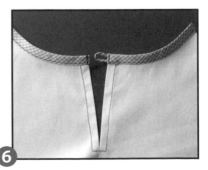

4 Loop turned right-side out.

5 Fold end of bias tape under by ⅜ in (1cm). Trim other end to desired length, fold and pin in position.

6 Sew into place.

(RS)

How to Attach Tape **applied pattern 3 → p.27**

Tape or ribbon gives a cute accent even to simple fabric.

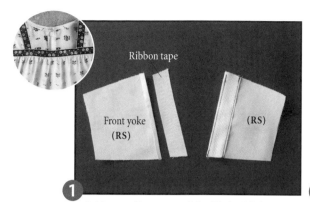

1 Fold seam allowance to right side for fabric to which ribbon tape will be attached. Cut ribbon tape to desired length (left). Place tape over fabric and stitch both edges.

2 Gather upper edge of yoke. Conceal gathering stitches by placing ribbon tape over the top and sewing into place.

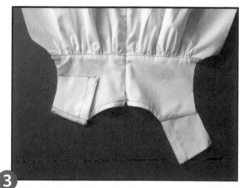

3 Bind back neckline using bias tape. Sew shoulders and press seams toward back.

4 Place front over yoke pieces and sew over upper edge of ribbon tape.

 Using Tulle **applied pattern 6b → p.33**

Tulle is a fine net fabric with hexagon-shaped holes. When cutting tulle, no seam allowance is necessary.

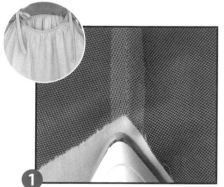

1 Sew edges together and open out seam. High temperatures damage synthetic tulle, so place a cloth over tulle and use a low heat setting when ironing.

2 Gather neckline of front of dress and tulle layer together. Bind armholes and neckline with bias tape.

3 Only the neckline and armholes are bound to the main garment with bias tape; the rest of the tulle is left free.

✂ How to Attach a Frill   applied pattern 1a, 1b → p.23   applied pattern 5 → p.31

Gathering and attaching a frill to a hem.

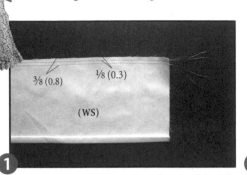

① ⅜ (0.8)   ⅛ (0.3)   (WS)

Make two rows of stitches along the side of the frill to be gathered (⅛ in and ⅜ in [0.8cm and 0.3cm] from edge). Press the hem up in a double fold.

② Divide both the side of the frill to be attached and the hem of the garment into four equal sections and mark symbols.

③ Match right sides of frill and garment, matching symbols. Pin in place. Pull up gathering stitches so frill is same width as bottom edge of garment.

④ Sew through both layers with the frill on top. Use an awl to distribute gathers evenly as the fabric moves through the machine.

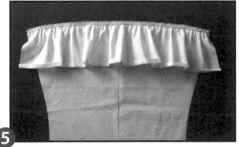

⑤ The stitched frill.

⑥ Finish off the seam allowance by sewing through both layers with a zigzag stitch.

① Press seam towards garment. Sew ¼ in (0.7cm) from edge of garment on right side of fabric to keep seam in place.

② Sew side seam, including frill. Press side seam towards back.

③ Sew hem in a double fold.

⊙ Attaching a frill from above (1)

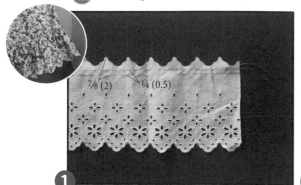

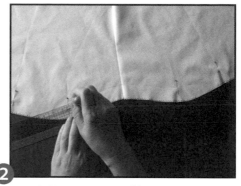

1 To emphasise the edging on a store-bought frill, make two rows of stitching along the edge to be attached.

2 Mark all around garment 1⅛ in (3cm) from hem using dressmaker's chalk. This allows you to place the top of the frill evenly 1⅛ in (3cm) up from the hem edge.

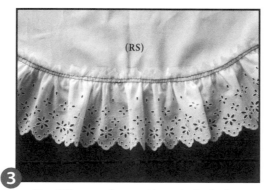

(RS)

3 Place frill on top of garment hem, pinning in place. Pull up gathering threads and distribute gathers evenly. Sew frill in place by stitching over both rows of gathering threads.

⊙ Attaching a frill from above (2)

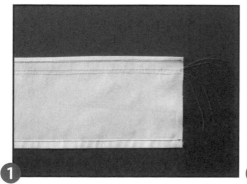

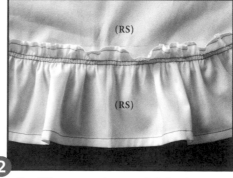

(RS)

(RS)

1 Hem the top and bottom of frill using a double fold. Create two rows of stitching along top of frill.

2 Sew frill to garment (see steps 2, 3 above).

Finishing Off a Neck Opening with a Facing

basic pattern 2 → p.24

Attaching a facing to finish off a neckline that fastens with a button at the back.

1 Apply fusible interfacing to back facing, ³⁄₈ in (1cm) in towards body of garment. Neaten edge of facing using a zigzag stitch.

2 Press hem seam allowance.

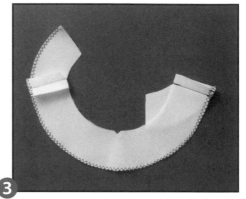

3 Use a zigzag stitch around outer edge of facing pieces. Match right sides of facing pieces and sew at shoulders. Press seams open.

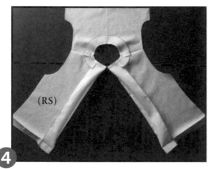

4 Sew garment shoulder seams and press seams towards back. Turn back facings right side out. Match right sides of facing and garment, matching symbols at center front and shoulders. (The back neck facing will overlap the back facing by ³⁄₈ in (1cm) on each side.) Sew neckline. Sew hem of back facing to garment also.

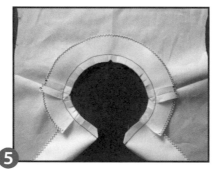

5 Clip curves at ³⁄₈ in (1cm) intervals, being careful not to cut into stitching. Trim off corners of back facing on the diagonal to decrease bulk when turning.

6 Trim edge of hem on diagonal also. Trim off back facing hem to leave a ³⁄₈ in (1cm) seam allowance.

7 Iron along stitching line, pressing seam allowance in towards facing. This achieves a crisp finish when the facing is turned right side out.

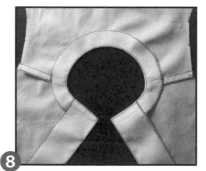

8 Turn facing right side out and press again. Sew back facing and neck facing in a continuous seam ¹⁄₁₆ in (0.1cm) from edge.

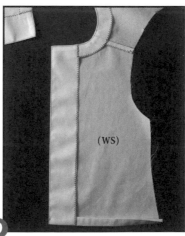

9 The finished neckline with the back edge in place.

Attaching a collar (1) applied pattern **2a** → p.25

This design has a small collar and a partially elasticized neckline.

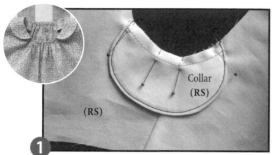

1 Create collar (see p49) and pin in position on neckline. Baste in place using ⅜ in (0.8cm) stitches.

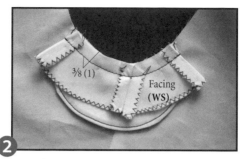

2 Sew facing sections together at shoulders (see p46) and fold ends under by ⅜ in (1cm). Match right sides of neckline from step 1 and sew. Trim seam allowance to ¼ in (0.5cm).

3 Match right sides of garment from step 2 with bias tape (see p18. Trim tape so it overlaps facing by about ⅜ in [1cm]) and sew. Clip curves at about ⅜ in(1cm) intervals.

4 Turn right side out and sew bias tape in place. Pin a safety pin to the end of the indicated length of elastic to pass it under bias tape.

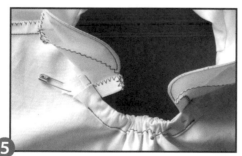

5 Pin the start of the elastic to secure it, passing the end out.

6 Pin end of elastic to secure it.

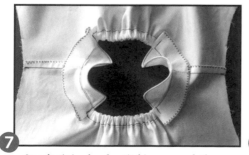

7 Sew elastic in place by stitching over ends three times through facing.

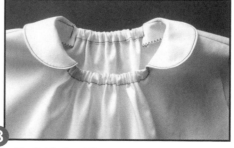

8 The finished neckline.

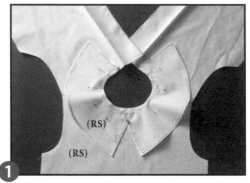

1 Create collar. Match at center front and pin in place with right collar over left.

(RS)

(RS)

🔘 Attaching a collar (2)   applied pattern **2b** → p.25

This design shows a big collar which overlaps at the front.

2 Fold back facings to right side. Create facing (see p46). Match right side of facing and garment and pin in place.

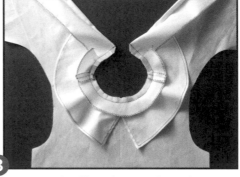

3 Sew around neckline. Clip curves (see p46).

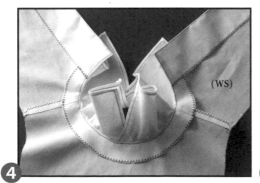

4 Fold facing to wrong side of garment (see p46). Sew to neckline 1/16 in (0.1cm) from edge, making sure not to catch collar in stitching.

5 The finished collar.

(WS)

🔘 Attaching a collar (3)   ⟨ applied pattern 7 → p.34 ⟩

A collar like this one with no neck band is called a flat collar.

1 Match right sides of collar pieces and sew around outer edge.

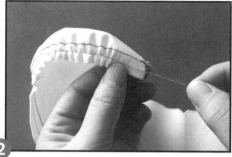

2 In the seam allowance, sew a line of gathering stitches ¼ in (0.4cm) from edge. Pull up stitches to match the rounded shape of the collar.

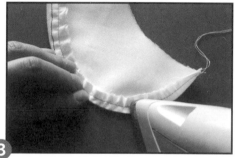

3 Press seam allowance in to upper side of collar along stitching line from step 1 (flatten gathering with iron).

4 The collar with outer edge pressed in.

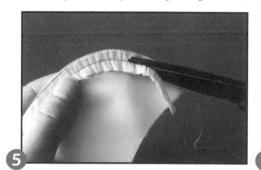

5 Trim off excess seam allowance, cutting just inside gathering stitches.

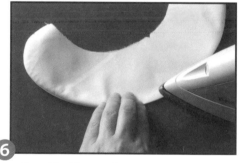

6 Turn right side out and press.

7 Sew around edge 1/16 in (0.1cm) from edge.

(continued from p49)

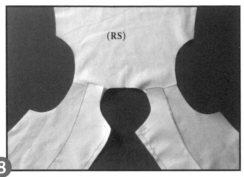

8 Sew shoulders of garment and press seams towards back. Match right sides of garment and front facings and sew from endpoint of collar down front edges.

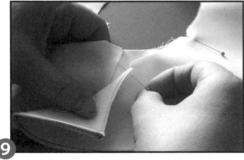

9 Pin collar to garment, matching symbols at endpoints of collar at front, center backs and shoulder seams.

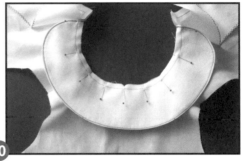

10 Avoiding front facings, baste collar ⅜ in (0.8cm) from edge between collar endpoint symbols.

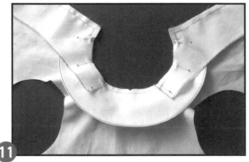

11 Layer front facings over top of collar and pin.

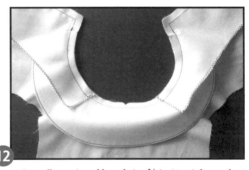

12 Sew collar section of front facing ⅜ in (1cm) from edge.

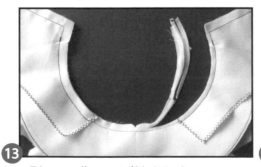

13 Trim seam allowance to ¼ in (0.5cm).

14 Pin bias tape (see p18) around collar between front facings, leaving ⅜ in (1cm) at each end to overlap front facings.

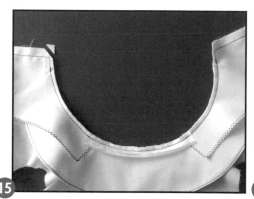

15 Sew section with bias tape ¼ in (0.5cm) from edge. Trim corners of front facings on the diagonal. Clip curves and press facing towards garment.

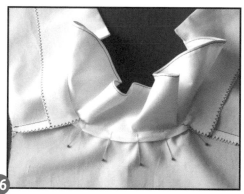

16 Turn facing and bias tape right side out and pin.

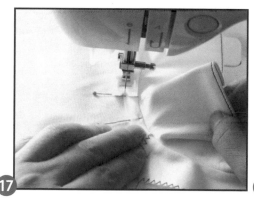

17 Sew bias tape ¹⁄₁₆ in (0.1cm) from edge, being careful not to catch collar in stitching.

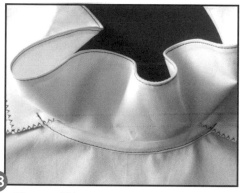

18 The secured bias tape.

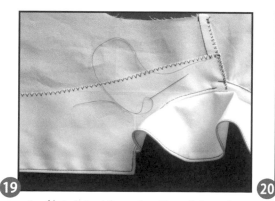

19 Sew ¹⁄₁₆ in (0.1cm) from edge of front facing and neckline section. Attach shoulder of front facing to garment shoulder using blind hem stitch.

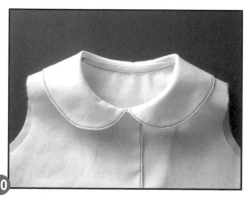

20 The completed collar.

Attaching a Sleeve

This sleeve has gathers on the sleeve cap and elasticized cuffs and is known as a puff sleeve.

 How to attach a sleeve (1)   basic pattern 2 → p.24   applied pattern 2a → p.25

In this method, the cap of the sleeve is attached to the garment, and the underside of the sleeve and side of garment are sewn in a continuous seam.

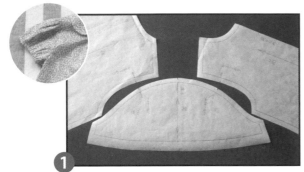

1 Check that symbols for shoulder lines and endpoints of gathering on garment front, back and sleeves are correct and transfer markings to fabric (see p10).

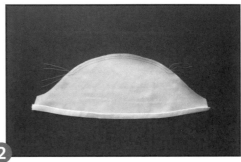

2 Sew two parallel rows of gathering stitches around sleeve cap and press up sleeve opening in a double fold.

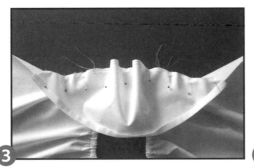

3 Match right sides of garment and sleeve and pin in place. Make sure shoulder lines, sides and gathering endpoint match.

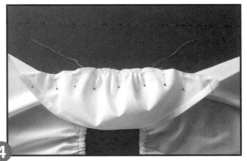

4 Pull up gathering threads and distribute gathers evenly.

5 Sew sleeve to garment. Sew through both layers of seam allowance using zigzag stitch (see steps 4–6 on p44).

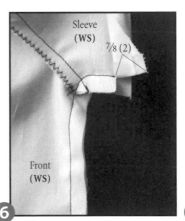

Sleeve (WS)

⅞ (2)

Front (WS)

6 Sew underside of sleeve and side in continuous seam, leaving ⅞ in (2cm) at sleeve opening. Clip seam allowance of seam front and open out (this will form casing for elastic).

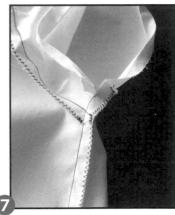

7 Sew through both layers of seam allowance using zigzag stitch and press seam towards back.

8 Turn sleeve opening back in a double fold and sew. Insert elastic (see step 4 on p47).

9 Overlap ends of elastic by ⅞ in (2cm) and stitch three times.

10 The finished sleeve.

How to attach a sleeve (2)   applied pattern **2b** → p.25

This design uses elastic just above the sleeve opening to look like a frill.

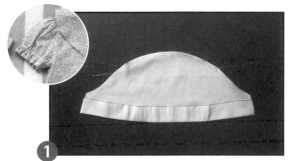

1 Make two rows of gathering stitches around sleeve cap. Sew along sleeve opening using zigzag stitch and press up in a single fold.

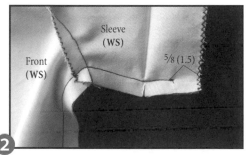

2 Attach sleeve to garment (see steps 3–5 on p52). Leave ⅝ in (1.5cm) at sleeve opening and sew underside of sleeve and side in a continuous seam. Clip seam allowance of sleeve front at crease made by iron.

Sleeve (WS)
Front (WS)
⅝ (1.5)

3 Sew through both layers of seam allowance using zigzag stitch and press seam towards back. Open out seam allowance from clip mark (this will form casing for elastic).

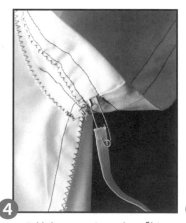

4 Fold sleeve opening and sew ⅞ in (2cm) and 1⅛ in (3cm) from edge. Insert elastic through casing (see step 4 on p47).

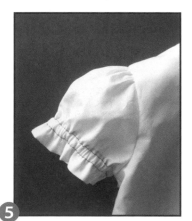

5 The finished sleeve.

● How to attach a sleeve with cuffs   basic pattern 3 → p.26

For a sleeve with cuffs, create the sleeve and sew body of garment and sides before attaching sleeves.

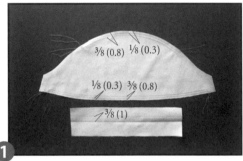

1 Create two rows of gathering stitches around sleeve cap and sleeve edge (¹⁄₈ and ³⁄₈ in [0.8 and 0.3 cm] from edge). Apply fusible interfacing up to ³⁄₈ in (1cm) into outer side of cuff. Fold in half to create crease.

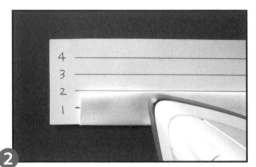

2 Place ironing ruler along halfway mark crease and press under outer side of cuff to ⁷⁄₈ in (2cm) mark.

3 Fold seam allowance of opposite side of cuff (inner side) over fold created in step 2.

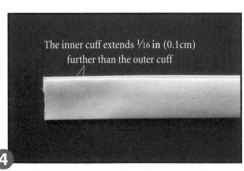

The inner cuff extends ¹⁄₁₆ in (0.1cm) further than the outer cuff

4 Folding inner side of cuff in this way makes it about ¹⁄₁₆ in (0.1cm) wider than the outer side of cuff, so it's certain that stitches will go through it even when sewing from outer side of cuff.

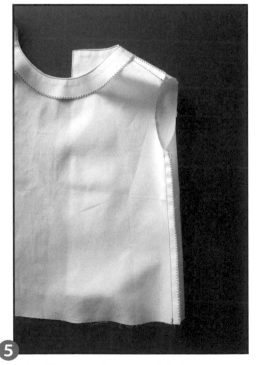

5 Sew side seams and press towards back.

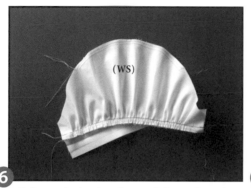

6 Pull up gathering threads around sleeve edge and sew to right side of cuff. Press seam towards cuff.

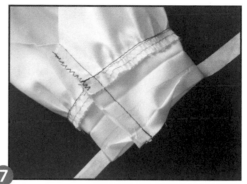

7 Sew underside of sleeve and cuff in a continuous seam and press seam towards back. Apply heat-fusible double-sided tape to seam allowance of inner cuff (see p15).

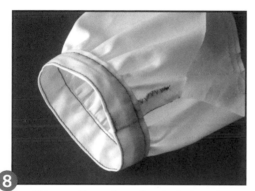

8 Fold inner cuff up and sew along both edges of cuff from outer side.

9 Match right sides of garment and sleeve and pin at shoulders, underside of sleeve and endpoints of gathers. Pull up gathering threads and distribute evenly and sew sleeve to garment.

10 The finished garment.

Finishing Off an Armhole with a Facing

basic pattern 7 → p.34   applied pattern 7 → p.35

Using facings on the armholes of a sleeveless blouse creates a neat finish.

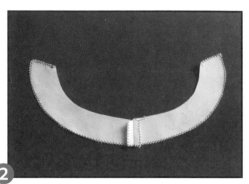

1 Use zigzag stitch to stitch around outer edges of facings. Apply fusible interfacing to both front and back facings.

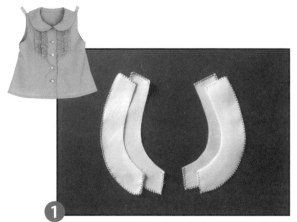

2 Sew shoulders and press seam towards back.

3 Match right sides of garment and facing at shoulders and sew around armhole. Clip curves at ⅜ in (1cm) intervals.

(RS)

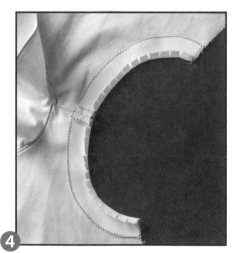

4 Press seam allowance towards facing along stitching line.

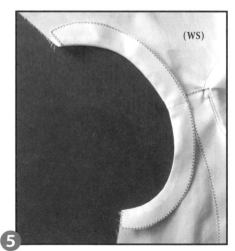

(WS)

5 Turn facing to wrong side and press.

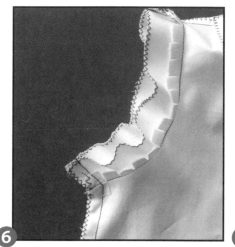

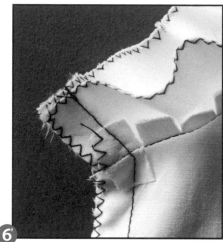

6 Sew from facing along side in a continuous seam, finishing seam allowance with a zigzag stitch. Press seam towards back.

6' Close up detail showing facing seam opened out before sewing side seam.

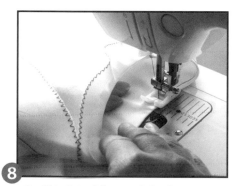

7 Press neatly.

8 Sew ¼ in (0.5cm) from armhole edge.

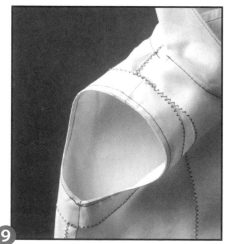

9 Secure facing at shoulder and side using blind hem stitch (see p41).

⤜ How to Sew Pants basic pattern 4 → p.28

These instructions are for pants with an elastic waist. The sewing method is the same regardless of the pants length.

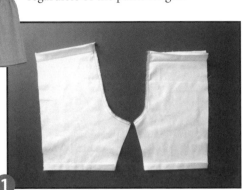

1 Using an ironing ruler, press hems and waist of both pants front (right) and pants back (left—note the longer crotch) to create double folds. Match right sides of pants front sections and sew crotch. Do the same for pants back sections. (Leave seam allowance free for pants back as this will form the opening for the elastic casing.) Press seams towards what will be the left of the pants when they are complete (press open the casing opening).

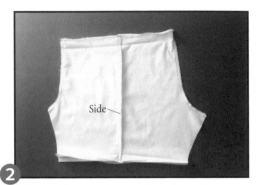

2 Match right sides of pants sides and sew side seams. Press seams towards back.

3 Sew inside leg in a continuous seam and press towards back.

4 Double fold waist and sew ¹⁄₁₆ in (0.1cm) from edge that has been turned to inside pants. Sew again between this stitching line and waist edge.

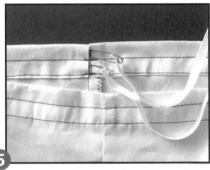

5 Insert elastic through both casings simultaneously, using safety pins to pull elastic through.

1 Guide safety pins through using both hands for an even result.

2 Finish off elastic (see step 9 on p53) to complete pants.

How to Sew Shirring Elastic

basic pattern 5 → p.30   applied pattern 5 → p.31

Wind shirring elastic around the bobbin and sew to create shirring.

1 Using water soluble dressmaker's chalk, rule parallel lines on right side of fabric to indicate position of shirring.

2 Wind shirring elastic around bobbin, pulling slightly as you go.

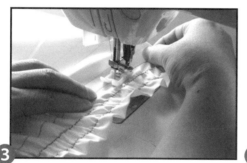

3 Pull fabric taut as you sew.

4 Pull shirring elastic at sides and adjust to correct measurements.

5 Pull shirring elastic to draw upper threads to wrong side of material.

6 Tie ends of shirring elastic together twice, then knot both strands together.

7 Fasten sewing threads in same way.

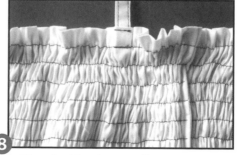

8 Trim ends of thread to about ⅜ in (1cm) to finish.

How to Sew Overalls applied pattern 4 → p.29

These overalls have shoulder straps and a bib with a pocket. The back waist is elasticized for ease of wear.

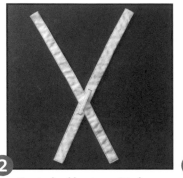

1 Apply fusible tape to pocket opening at pants front.

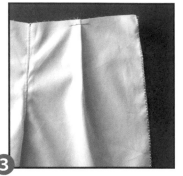

2 Create shoulder straps. Attach shoulder strap keeper to one strap.

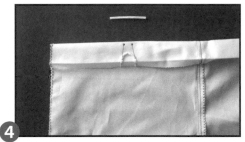

3 Sew front crotch and press seam towards left side of pants. Create tucks and stitch in place in seam allowance.

4 Sew back crotch and press seam towards left side of pants. Make double fold on back of pants waist. Create a 1⅞ in (4.5cm) long fabric loop (see p42) and pin in position.

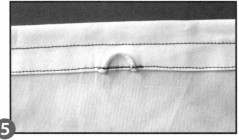

5 Sew back waist to pants 1/16 in (0.1cm) from folded under edge. Sew another row of stitching between first row and waist edge. Press fabric loop up and sew over stitching along folded under edge of waist casing.

6 Insert two lengths of elastic through waist casings (see p58) and sew to sides to secure.

7 Sew shoulder straps to right side of outer bib.

sew to point where garment will be completed

8 Match right sides of outer and inner bib pieces and sew around sides and top, leaving base free.

9 Turn right side out and press. Fold under ⅜ in (1cm) along base of inner bib.

10 Match right sides of outer bib and pants front and sew together. Avoid catching inner side of bib in stitching.

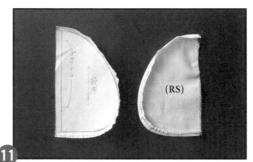

11 Sew gathering stitches around curves on pockets. Cut pocket shape from thick card and place on pocket piece. Pull up gathering threads to match cardboard shape (left). Press seam allowance to right side (right).

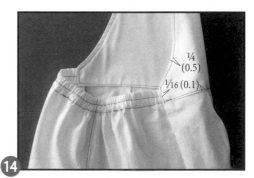

12 Match right sides of pants front and back and sew from outer bib along side, leaving pocket opening free.

13 Sandwich back waist section under inner side of bib and sew sides.

14 Turn inner side of bib right side out and sew at sides and along front waist 1/16 in (0.1cm) from edge and around bib 1/4 in (0.5cm) from edge.

15 Open out side seam and sew 1/4 in (0.5cm) from front pocket opening.

16 Sew straight side of pocket to pants back seam allowance, making sure not to catch front in stitching.

17 Flatten out and stitch around curve of pocket through pocket and pants front.

18 On right side of garment, stitch over top and bottom of pocket opening three times.

How to Insert an Invisible Zipper

basic pattern 3 → p26   applied pattern 3 → p.27

At first glance, this looks difficult, but if you sew according to the instructions it's easy—and gives a beautiful result.

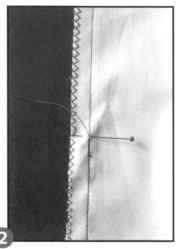

1 Apply fusible tape to seam allowance of center back opening where zipper is to be inserted.

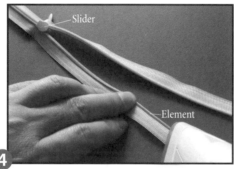

2 Sew center back seam from end of opening to hem (ie below pin). Above pin, where zipper is to go and sew seam with long stitches. Open out seam.

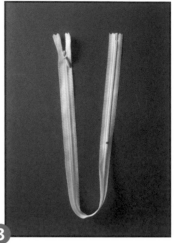

3 Prepare an invisible zipper more than 7/8 in (2cm) longer than measurement of zipper opening.

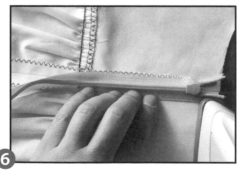

4 Use an iron on medium heat to flatten out teeth of zipper. An iron on high heat will damage the zipper, so take care.

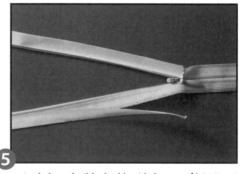

5 Apply heat-fusible double-sided tape to 3/8 in (1cm) before closure on outer side of zipper.

6 Close zipper. Match garment seam allowance with taped side of zipper and iron to secure.

7 Remove long stitches from step 2 and bring zipper head down to gap at end of seam.

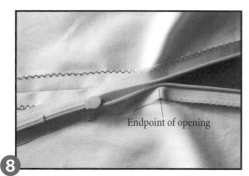

8 The open zipper.

Endpoint of opening

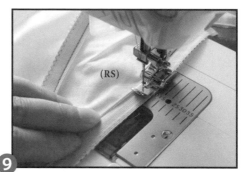

9 Using a zipper foot, sew zipper to end of opening. Make sure the needle sews as close to the zipper teeth as possible.

(RS)

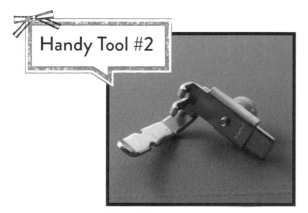

Zipper foot

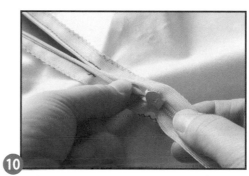

10 Close zipper (this is important because otherwise the zipper will not be able to be opened or closed).

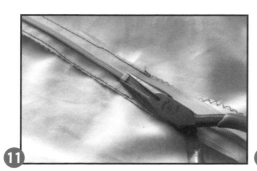

11 Once the zipper is sewn to seam allowance, move clasp to position of seam opening and use pliers to secure in place so it doesn't move.

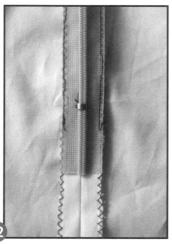

12 Trim 1⅛–1⅝ in (3–4cm) of end of zipper below clasp.

13 The finished zipper.

How to Attach a Hook and Eye basic pattern 3 → p26   applied pattern 3 → p.27

When a garment has an opening with a zipper, attaching a hook and eye at the top will keep the zipper closed.

1 A hook and eye set comprises a loop (left) and a hook (right).

2 On the wrong side of the back right of the garment, about ⅛ in (0.2cm) from the edge, hold the hook in place and insert the needle from underneath the fabric.

3 Stitch over the bar section of the hook 2–3 times to secure it.

4 Insert the needle from the outside of one hole to the inside, catching the thread.

5 Pull the needle through, catching the thread to form a buttonhole stitch. Repeat several times and for the other hole.

6 Place the eye section over the hook to check positioning, then sew eye to garment as per hook.

7 The finished result.

How to Sew a Smock  basic pattern 6 → p.32

This smock with an elasticized neckline can easily be worn to cover and protect other clothing and is comfortable as playwear or for mealtimes.

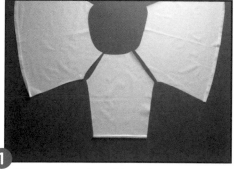

1 When cutting and attaching raglan sleeves to a garment, make sure not to confuse the front and back of the garment. Match right sides of garment and sleeves and sew from neck to underarm. Press seams towards body sections.

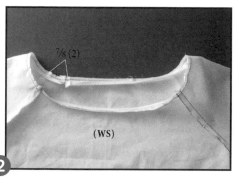

2 Create bias tape (see p18). Match right sides of neckline and bias tape and sew, starting about $7/8$ in (2cm) from back shoulder join and folding over $3/8$ in (1cm) at each end of bias tape for a neat finish.

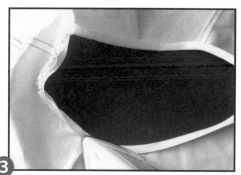

3 Clip seam allowance and iron to wrong side along stitching line.

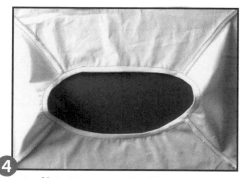

4 Sew $1/16$ in (0.1cm) around neckline.

5 Sew underside of sleeve and side seams in a continuous seam, leaving opening for casing at sleeve opening.

6 Insert elastic through neckline and sleeve openings (see p53). Double-fold hem and sew.

How to Sew a Partial Opening applied pattern 7 → p.35

It's easy to sew a partial opening on the front of a garment if a facing is used.

1 Apply fusible interfacing to facing and zigzag stitch around outer edge. Match right sides of facing and garment front and sew from collar endpoint to opening endpoint. Clip curves of seam allowance around opening.

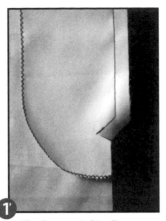

1' Clip close to stitching line, making sure not to cut through stitches.

2 Clip seam allowance at endpoint of collar in the same way.

3 Press seam towards facing along stitching line.

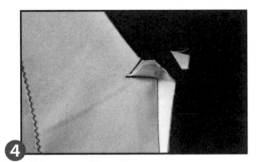

4 Trim corners diagonally.

5 Fold seam allowance and hold in place while turning right side out.

6 Use an awl to neaten corners.

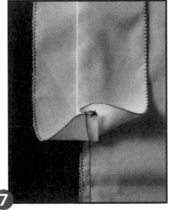

7 Sew center front of garment, zigzag stitching through both layers to finish. Sew center front of facing.

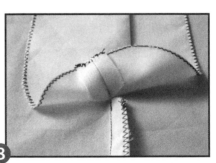

8 Press garment seam to right-hand side. Press facing seam open.

(as viewed from the right side of fabric)   (as viewed from the wrong side of fabric)

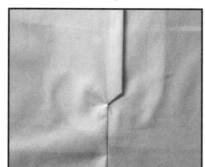

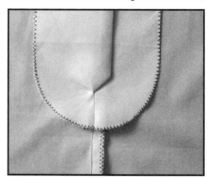

9 The opening finished off with a facing.

10 The endpoints of the left and right sides of a collar. The sailor collar attaches to these points.

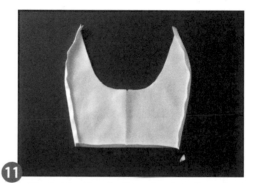

11 Match right sides of collar and under collar and sew. Press along stitching line and trim off corners diagonally. Turn right side out and sew around outer edge ¼ in (0.5cm) from edge.

12 Attach collar to neckline and finish off using facing and bias tape (see p50, 51). Sew around neckline to endpoint of opening ¹⁄₁₆ in (0.1cm) from edge.

13 Sew a triangle at opening endpoint for reinforcement.

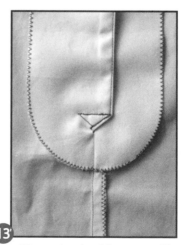

13' The opening viewed from wrong side of fabric. Blind hem stitch the bottom of the facing to the center front seam allowance to hold in place.

How to Do Smocking basic pattern 3 → p.26   applied pattern 3 → p.27

Embroidering over the top of gathered fabric is known as smocking. If you use gingham check fabric, the check pattern serves as a guide, so it's simple.

 Using gingham check

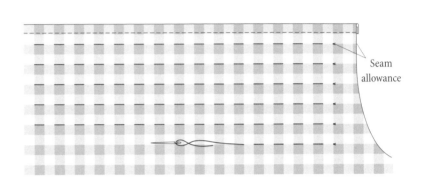

Seam allowance

1 Double-fold upper edge and sew. Use #30 machine sewing thread to sew by hand horizontally through section to be smocked, one stitch per square and in rows two squares apart.

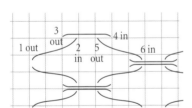

2 Pull up threads tightly and press using steam.

3 When fabric has dried, open out to indicated size and distribute gathers evenly.

4 Create embroidery using checks as a guide. Refer to the diagram above and insert the needle in and out from right to left in the order given, starting at 1. Once stitch is completed take needle one square up and pass from right to left through fold.

Pass needle out and pick up next edge of fold. Repeat to complete one row of embroidery.

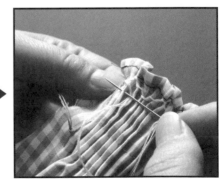

For the second row, work stitching by picking up folds one square below (ie work in a mirror image of first row).

4 continued

Pick up the next edge of fold.

Draw thread firmly to keep folds evenly spaced.

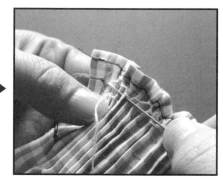

Alternate the stitches in the row being worked with those in the preceding row.

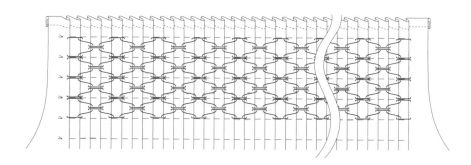

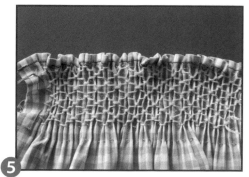

5 The completed embroidery.

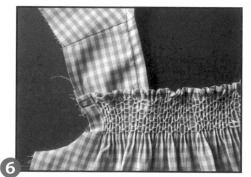

6 Sew front and back yokes at shoulders and finish off neckline using bias tape. Attach front to yoke.

● For plain fabric   applied pattern 3 → p.27

When smocking on plain fabric, the fabric must be marked for guidance.

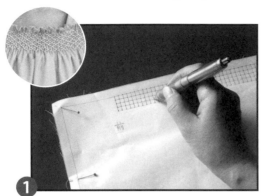

1 Place pattern over fabric and pin to secure. Using an automatic pencil, mark points where lines intersect on smocking graph, pressing firmly.

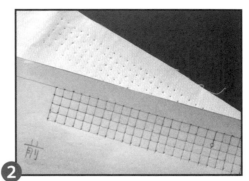

2 The intersecting points marked on the fabric.

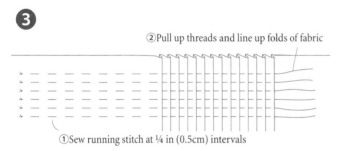

3

②Pull up threads and line up folds of fabric

①Sew running stitch at ¼ in (0.5cm) intervals

Pass needle through marked points and draw up threads

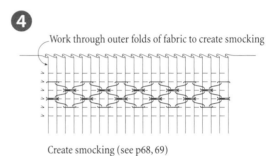

4 Work through outer folds of fabric to create smocking

Create smocking (see p68, 69)

How to Make a Pocket   basic pattern 6 → p.32

When making a round pocket, use card to create the curved shape.

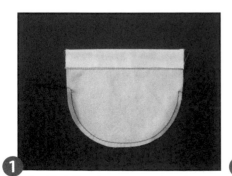

1 Double-fold pocket opening and sew (see p15). Sew gathering stitches around curve, ¼ in (0.5cm) from edge.

2 Trace pocket shape onto card (about the thickness of a postcard) and cut out. Place card template on wrong side of pocket and draw up threads to create shape.

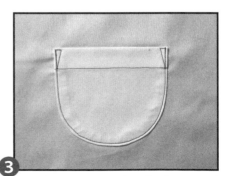

3 Attach to garment as indicated and sew around pocket ¹⁄₁₆ in (0.1cm) from edge (see p16).

[Applied Pattern 1a]

page 23

Full-size pattern piece side A

MATERIALS

【Materials required are the same for all 5 sizes unless otherwise indicated】

FABRIC

Plain cotton, 45 in (110cm) wide
for child 39½ in (100cm) tall: ½ yd (50cm);
 43½ in (110cm) tall: ⅝ yd (60cm);
 47½, 51¼ in (120, 130cm) tall:
 ¾ yd (70cm); 55 in (140cm) tall: ⅞ yd (80cm)
striped cotton, 45 in (110cm) wide
for child 39½, 43½ in (100, 110cm) tall: ¾ yd (70cm);
 47¼, 51¼ in (120, 130cm) tall: ⅞ yd (80cm);
 55 in (140cm) tall: 1⅛ yd (1m)
Striped ribbon: 1 in wide x 20 in (2.5cm wide x 50cm)
Heart-shaped button: ⅝ in (1.5cm) diameter x 1

INSTRUCTIONS

Preparation: *M stitch along center back edges

1 Create pockets and attach (see p70)
2 Create decoration from striped ribbon and attach
3 Sew center back and back opening (see p42)
4 Gather hem frill and attach to front and back of dress (see p44). M stitch through both layers of seam allowance. (For size 55 in [140cm] frill, sew three pieces together and gather, then attach to dress after side seams have been sewn)
5 Sew shoulders (see p18). M stitch through both layers of seam allowance
6 Create fabric loop (see p42. Trim to 2¼ in [5.5cm] long) and attach in position. Bind neckline with bias tape (see p18, 19)
7 Sew sides (see p21). M stitch through both layers of seam allowance
8 Bind armholes with bias tape (see p18, 19)
9 Double fold hem and sew
10 Attach button (see p39)

 *M = use a zigzag stitch to neaten seam allowance

Cutting layout (plain cotton)

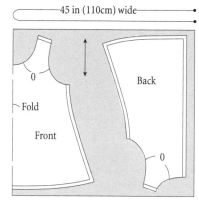

*Seam allowances are ⅜ in (1cm) unless otherwise indicated

Cutting layout (striped cotton)

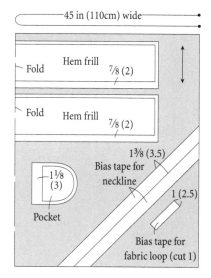

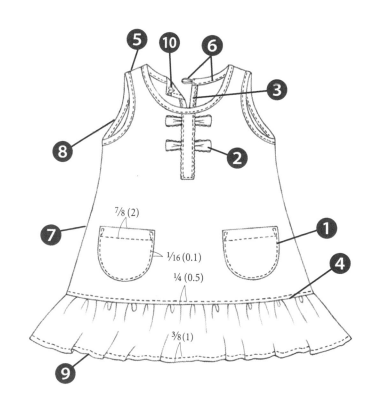

2

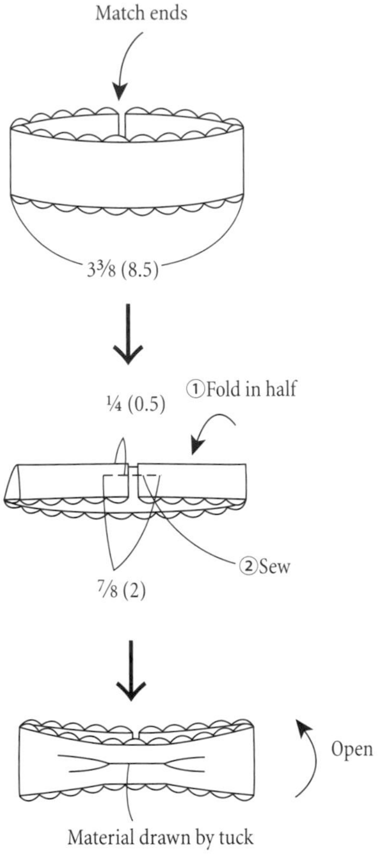
Match ends
3 3/8 (8.5)
1/4 (0.5)
①Fold in half
7/8 (2)
②Sew
Open
Material drawn by tuck

Drafting

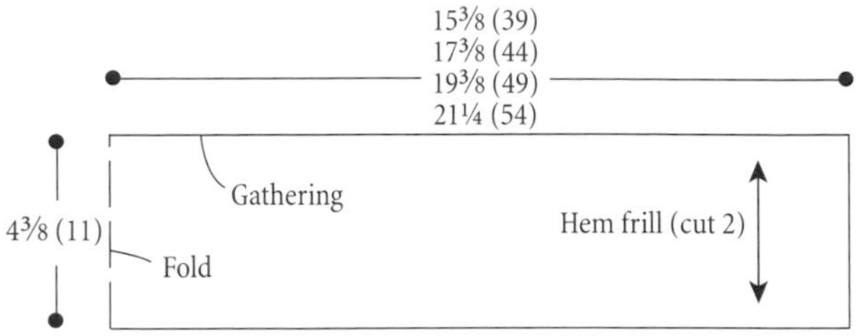
15 3/8 (39)
17 3/8 (44)
19 3/8 (49)
21 1/4 (54)
4 3/8 (11)
Gathering
Fold
Hem frill (cut 2)

* The four measurements given are for children 39 1/2, 43 1/2, 47 1/4, 51 1/4 in (100, 110, 120, 130cm)

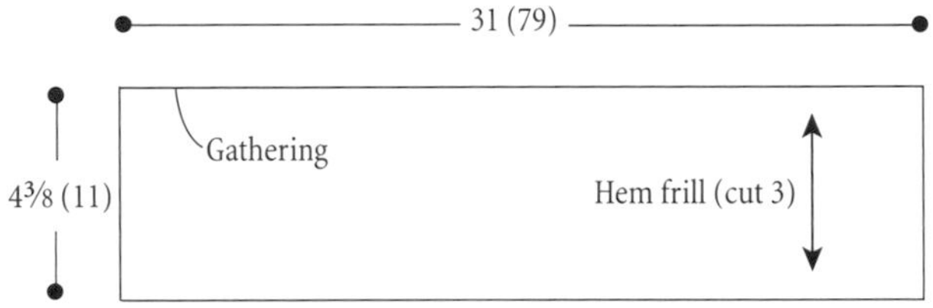
31 (79)
4 3/8 (11)
Gathering
Hem frill (cut 3)

* For a child 55 in (140cm) tall, join 3 hem frill pieces

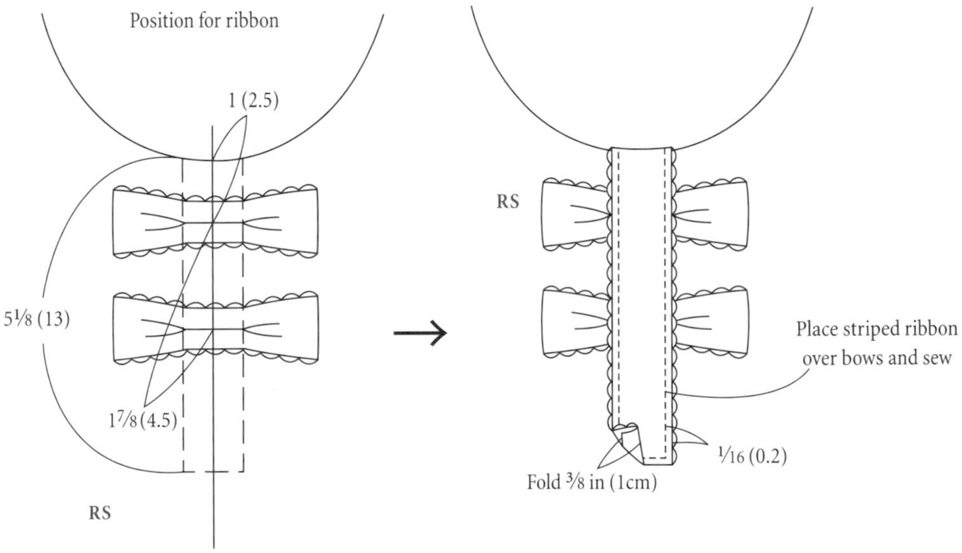
Position for ribbon
1 (2.5)
5 1/8 (13)
1 7/8 (4.5)
RS
RS
Place striped ribbon over bows and sew
1/16 (0.2)
Fold 3/8 in (1cm)

[Applied Pattern 1b]

page 23

Full-size pattern piece side A

MATERIALS

[Materials required are the same for all 5 sizes unless otherwise indicated]

FABRIC

Liberty print 45 in (110cm) wide
for child 39½ in (100cm) tall: ¾ yd (70cm); 43½ (110cm) tall: 7/8 yd (80cm); 47¼ in (120cm) tall: 1 yd (90cm); 51¼ in (130cm) tall: 1¼ yd (1m 10cm); 55 in (140cm) tall: 1½ yd (1m 40cm)

Scallop-edged tape (Liberty print, for hem frill) 4⅜ in (11cm) wide
for child 39½ in (100cm) tall: 1¾ yd (1m 60cm); for 43½ (110cm) tall: 2 yd (1m 80cm); for 47¼ in (120cm) tall: 2⅛ yd (2m); for 51¼ in (130cm) tall: 2⅜ yd (2m 20cm); for 55 in (140cm) tall: 2⅝ yd (2m 40cm)

Heart-shaped buttons: ⅝ in (1.5cm) diameter x 4

INSTRUCTIONS

Preparation: *M stitch center back edges and front and back of dress hem

1 Sew center back and back opening (see p42)
2 Sew shoulders (see p18). M stitch through both layers of seam allowance
3 Create fabric loop (see p42. Trim to 2¼ in [5.5cm] long) and attach. Complete neckline using bias tape (see p18, 20)
4 Bind armholes using bias tape (see p18, 20)
5 Sew sides (see p21). M stitch through both layers of seam allowance
6 Sew armholes (see p21)
7 Sew frill pieces together at sides. Create two rows of gathering stitches around frill
8 Attach frill to dress (see p45)
9 Attach buttons (see p39)

*M = use a zigzag stitch to neaten seam allowance

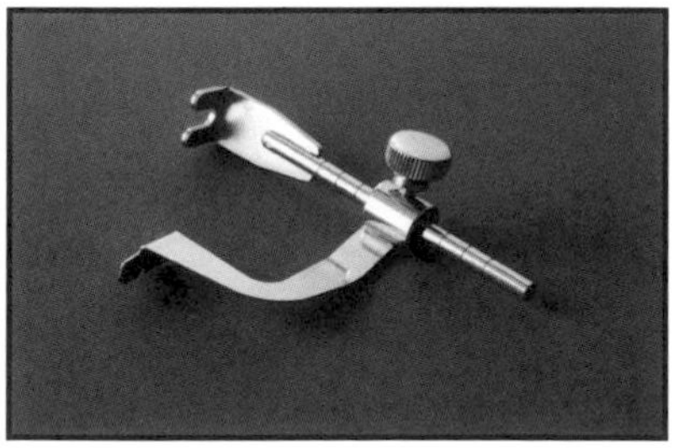

Stitch ruler

This tool attaches like a presser foot and allows you to sew stitches of the same length. Slide the width guide into position and secure in place. The guide is small so can even be used when sewing curves. (Please note: not all sewing machines are able to use stitch rulers)

Cutting layout

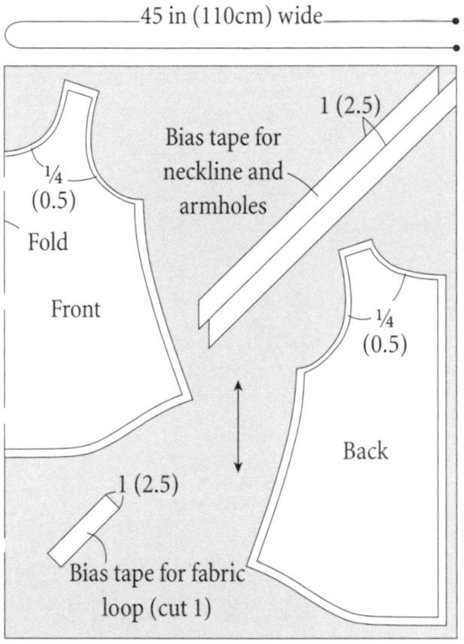

45 in (110cm) wide
1 (2.5)
Bias tape for neckline and armholes
¼ (0.5)
Fold
Front
¼ (0.5)
Back
1 (2.5)
Bias tape for fabric loop (cut 1)

*Seam allowances are ⅜ in (1cm) unless otherwise indicated

Drafting the hem frill

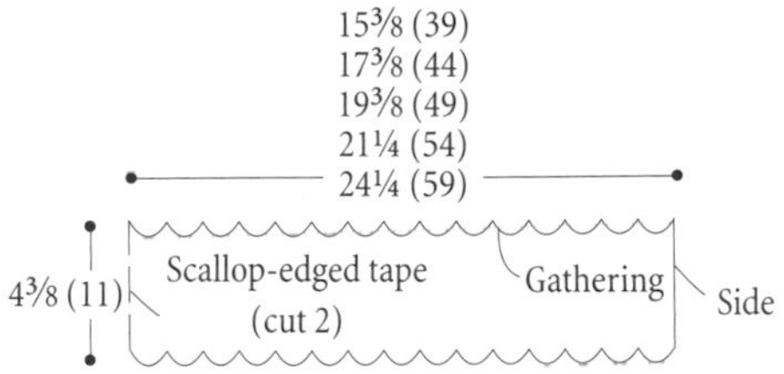

15⅜ (39)
17⅜ (44)
19⅜ (49)
21¼ (54)
24¼ (59)
4⅜ (11)
Scallop-edged tape (cut 2)
Gathering
Side

*Measurements are for children 39½, 43½, 47¼, 51¼, 55 in (100, 110, 120, 130,140cm) tall
*Side seam allowance is ⅜ in (1cm)

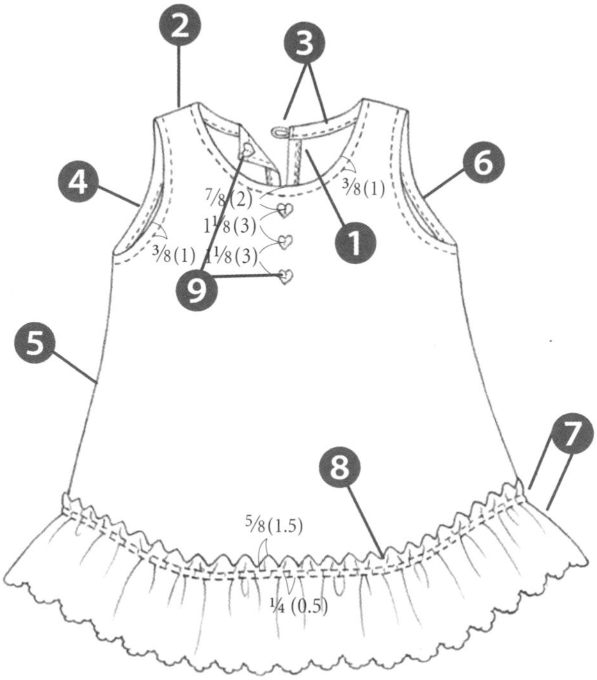

2
3
4
6
⅜ (1)
7/8 (2)
1⅛ (3)
1⅛ (3)
⅜ (1)
1
9
5
8
7
⅝ (1.5)
¼ (0.5)

[Basic Pattern 2]

page **24**

Full-size pattern piece side B

MATERIALS

【Materials required are the same for all 5 sizes unless otherwise indicated】

FABRIC

Cotton print 45 in (110cm) wide

for child 39½, 43½ in (100, 110cm) tall: ¾ yd (70cm); 47¼ in (120cm) tall:
⁷⁄₈ yd (80cm); 51¼ in (130cm) tall: 1 yd (90cm); 55 in (140cm) tall:
1⅛ yd (1m)

Fusible interfacing: for child 39½, 43½, 47¼ in (100, 110, 20cm) tall:
18 x 18 in (45 x 45cm); 130cm, 55 in (140cm) tall: 18 x 20 in (45 x 50cm)

Elastic ¼–⅜ in (8mm) wide

for child 39½ in (100cm) tall: 17⅜ in (44cm); 43½ in (110cm) tall: 18⅛ in (46cm);
47¼ in (120cm) tall: 19 in (48cm); 51¼ in (130cm) tall: 20 in (50cm);
55 in (140cm) tall: 21 in (52cm) (including seam allowance)

Heart-shaped buttons: ½ in (1.3cm) x 5

INSTRUCTIONS

Preparation: Apply adhesive interfacing to front and back neck facings and back
facing. *M stitch outer edge of facing and edge of back facing.

1 Sew shoulders (see p18). M stitch through both layers of seam allowance
2 Sew front and back neck facings together at shoulders and attach to neckline
   (see p46)
3 Sew around neckline and along edge of back facing
4 Gather sleeve caps and press sleeve openings in a double fold (see p52)
5 Pull up gathering threads and attach sleeves (see p52). M stitch through
   both layers of seam allowance
6 Leaving casing open on sleeve opening, sew underside of sleeves and
   side seams in continuous seam (see p52)
7 M stitch through both layers of seam allowance. Sew double-folded
   sleeve openings (see p40)
8 Insert elastic through casings (see p53)
9 Double-fold hem and sew (see p40). Create buttonholes and
   attach buttons (see p39)

   *M = use a zigzag stitch to neaten seam allowance

Cutting layout

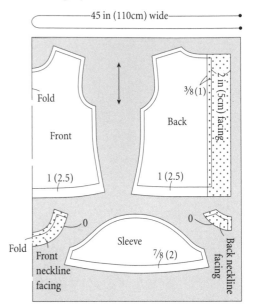

* Seam allowances are ⅜ in (1cm) unless otherwise
indicated

Shaded area indicates fusible interfacing

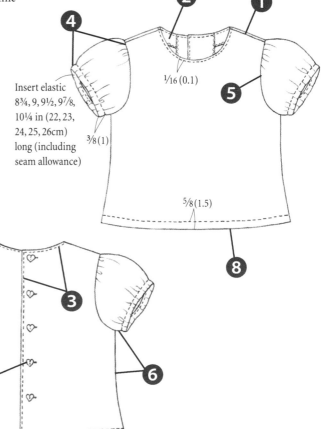

[Applied Pattern 2 a]

page 25

Full-size pattern piece side B

MATERIALS

[Materials required are the same for all 5 sizes unless otherwise indicated]

FABRIC

Cotton print 45 in (110cm) wide

for child 39½ in (100cm) tall: ⅞ yd (80cm); 43½ in (110cm) tall:
1 yd (90cm); 47¼ in (120cm) tall: 1⅛ yd (1m); 51¼ in (130cm) tall :
1¼ yd (1m 10cm); 55 in (140cm) tall: 1⅓ yd (1m 20cm)

Fusible interfacing: 36 x 8 in (90 x 20cm)

Elastic ¼–⅜ in (8mm) wide

for child 39½ in (100cm) tall: 26 in (66cm);
43½ in (110cm) tall: 27 in (68cm); 47¼ in (120cm) tall:
28 in (70cm); 51¼ in (130cm) tall: 29 in (72cm); 55 in (140cm) tall:
29 in (74cm) (including seam allowance)

INSTRUCTIONS

Preparation: Apply fusible interfacing to collar and front and back facings.
*M stitch around outer edges of facings

1 Sew shoulders (see p18). M stitch through both layers of seam allowance

2 Create collar (see p49) and attach in position (see p47). Sew front and back neck facings together at shoulders and attach to neckline (see p47)

3 Finish off parts of neckline where there is no facing using bias tape to form a casing. Insert elastic (see p47)

4 Gather sleeve caps and press sleeve openings in a double fold (see p52)

5 Pull up gathering threads and attach sleeves (see p52). M stitch through both layers of seam allowance

6 Leaving casing open on sleeve opening, sew underside of sleeves and side seams in continuous seam (see p52). M stitch through both layers of seam allowance

7 Sew double-folded sleeve openings (see p40) and insert elastic through casings (see p53)

8 Double-fold hem and sew (see p40).

    ＊M = use a zigzag stitch to neaten seam allowance

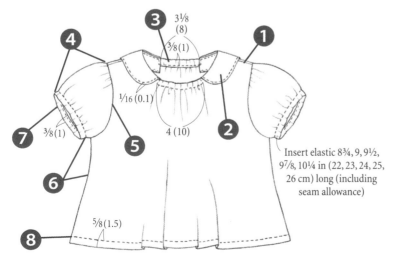

3⅛ (8)

⅜ (1)

1/16 (0.1)

4 (10)

⅜ (1)

⅝ (1.5)

Insert elastic 8¾, 9, 9½, 9⅞, 10¼ in (22, 23, 24, 25, 26 cm) long (including seam allowance)

Cutting layout

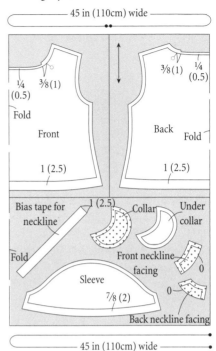

45 in (110cm) wide

¼ (0.5) ⅜ (1)   ⅜ (1) ¼ (0.5)

Fold

Front   Back Fold

1 (2.5)   1 (2.5)

Bias tape for neckline 1 (2.5) Collar Under collar

Fold   Front neckline facing 0

Sleeve ⅞ (2) 0

Back neckline facing

45 in (110cm) wide

＊Seam allowances are ⅜ in (1cm) unless otherwise indicated

[:::] Shaded area indicates fusible interfacing

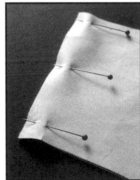

How to use pins

Match symbols on two pieces of fabric and insert pins perpendicular to stitching line. Pin first at seam start and finish, then pin between these points. If you are sewing a long seam, use more pins.

Bad Pinning

Fabric not matched up properly or pins at diagonal angles will result in an unattractive seam.

[Applied Pattern 2 b]

page 25

Full-size pattern piece side B

MATERIALS

【Materials required are the same for all 5 sizes unless otherwise indicated】

FABRIC

Liberty print 45 in (110cm) wide

for child 39½, 43½ in (100, 110cm) tall: 1 yd (90cm); 47¼ in (120cm) tall:
1⅛ yd (1m); 51¼ in (130cm) tall: 1¼ yd (1m 10cm); 55 in (140cm) tall:
1⅓ yd (1m 20cm)

Fusible interfacing: for child 39½, 43½, 47¼ in (100, 110, 120cm) tall:
18 x 18 in (45 x 45cm); 51¼, 55 in (130, 140cm) tall: 18 x 20 in (45 x 50cm)

Elastic ¼–⅜ in (8mm) wide

for child 39½ in (100cm) tall: 17⅜ in (44cm); 43½ in (110cm) tall:
18⅛ in (46cm); 47¼ in (120cm) tall: 19 in (48cm); 51¼ in (130cm) tall:
20 in (50cm); 55 in (140cm) tall: 21 in (52cm) (including seam allowance)

Self-cover buttons: ⅝ in (1.5cm) x 5

INSTRUCTIONS

Preparation: Apply adhesive interfacing to front and back neck facings and back
facing. *M stitch outer edge of facing, edge of back facing and sleeve openings.

1 Sew shoulders (see p18). M stitch through both layers of seam allowance
2 Double-fold edges of collar and sew. Attach front and back facings
to neckline
3 Sew around neckline and along edge of back facing
4 Sew gathering stitches around sleeve caps. Single-fold sleeve openings (see p53)
5 Pull up gathering stitches along sleeve caps and attach sleeves (see p52).
M stitch through both layers of seam allowance
6 Sew undersides of sleeves and side seams in continuous seam, leaving
casing open at sleeve opening (see p52). M stitch through both layers
of seam allowance
7 Sew single-folded sleeve openings (see p41) and insert elastic (see p53)
8 Double-fold hem and sew (see p40)
9 Create buttonholes and attach buttons (see p39)

　＊M = use a zigzag stitch to neaten seam allowance

Cutting layout

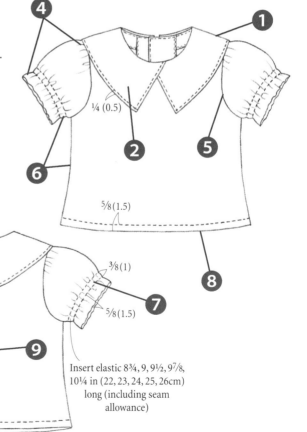

＊Seam allowances are ⅜ in (1cm) unless
otherwise indicated

▦ Shaded area indicates fusible interfacing

[Basic Pattern 3]

page 26

Full-size pattern side B, C

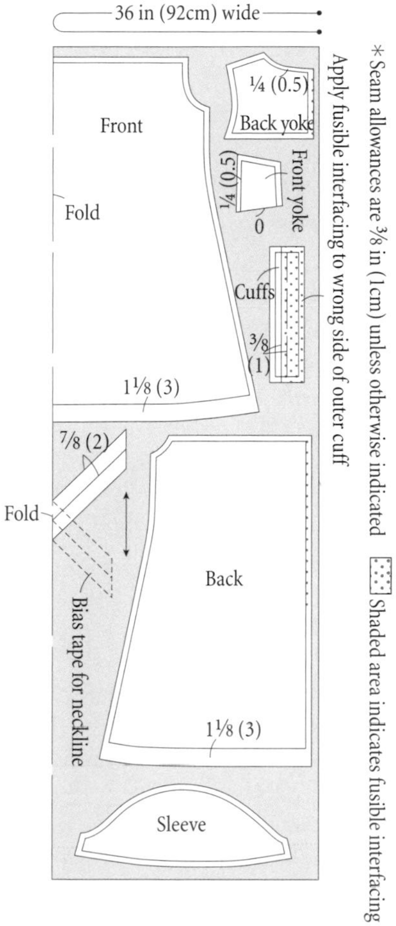

MATERIALS

【Materials required are the same for all 5 sizes unless otherwise indicated】

FABRIC

Gingham check 36 in (92cm) wide

for child 39½ in (100cm) tall: 1⅝ yd (1m 50cm); 43½ in (110cm) tall: 1⅞ yd (1m 70cm);
    47¼ in (120cm) tall: 2¼ yd (2m 10cm); 51¼ in (130cm) tall: 2⅜ yd (2m 20cm);
    55 in (140cm) tall: 2½ yd (2m 30cm)

Fusible interfacing: for 39½, 43½ in (100, 110cm) tall: 4 x 10 in (10 x 25cm);
    47¼, 51¼, 55 in (120, 130, 140cm): 4 x 12 in (10 x 30cm)

Fusible tape: ⅝ in (1.5cm) wide x 1 yd (90cm)

Invisible zipper: for 39½, 43½, 47¼ in (100, 110, 120cm) tall: 16 in (40cm) x 1;
    51¼, 55 in (130, 140cm) tall: 20 in (50cm) x 1

Hook and eye x 1 set

#25 embroidery thread as required

INSTRUCTIONS

Preparation: Apply fusible interfacing to outer cuffs and fusible tape at zipper position.

  *M stitch center back edges of back and back yoke and lower edge of front yoke pieces.

1 Double-fold seam allowance of upper edge of dress front (see p40)
2 Create smocking on dress front (see p68)
3 Pull up gathering stitches at dress back and attach back yoke
4 Sew center back seam to endpoint of zipper and insert invisible zipper (see p62)
5 Sew front and back yokes together at shoulders (see p18). M stitch through both layers of seam allowance
6 Finish off neckline using bias tape (see p18, 20)
7 Place front yoke under front of dress and sew (see p69)
8 Sew sides (see p54). M stitch through both layers of seam allowance
9 Sew gathering stitches around sleeve caps and along sleeve edges (see p54)
10 Pull up gathering threads and attach outer cuffs to sleeves. Sew undersides of sleeves, including cuffs (see p55). M stitch through both layers of seam allowance
11 Finish off cuffs (see p55)
12 Attach sleeves (see p55). M stitch through both layers of seam allowance
13 Double-fold hem and sew (see p40)
14 Attach hook and eye (see p64)

  * M = use a zigzag stitch to neaten seam allowance
  * Cutting layout shown is for size 36 in (92cm).
    For sizes 110–140cm, lay out pieces to suit

Cutting layout

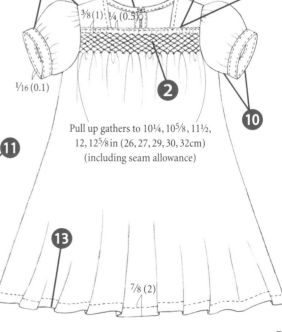

— 36 in (92cm) wide —

Front

Fold

¼ (0.5)
Back yoke

Front yoke
¼ (0.5)
0

Cuffs

⅜ (1)

1⅛ (3)

⅞ (2)

Fold

Bias tape for neckline

Back

1⅛ (3)

Sleeve

* Seam allowances are ⅜ in (1cm) unless otherwise indicated

Apply fusible interfacing to wrong side of outer cuff

⠿ Shaded area indicates fusible interfacing

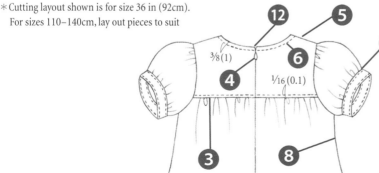

⅜ (1)   ¼ (0.5)

¹⁄₁₆ (0.1)

Pull up gathers to 10¼, 10⅝, 11½, 12, 12⅝ in (26, 27, 29, 30, 32cm) (including seam allowance)

⅜ (1)

¹⁄₁₆ (0.1)

⅞ (2)

［Applied Pattern 3］
page 27
Full-size pattern side B, C

MATERIALS
【Materials required are the same for all 5 sizes unless otherwise indicated】
FABRIC
Embroidered cotton 45 in (108cm) wide

for child 39½ in (100cm) tall: 1½ yd (1m 40cm); 43½ in (110cm) tall: 1¾ yd (1m 60cm);
  47¼ in (120cm) tall: 2 yd (1m 80cm); 51¼ in (130cm) tall: 2⅛ yd (2m);
  55 in (140cm) tall: 2⅜ yd (2m 20cm)

Fusible tape: ⅝ in (1.5cm) wide x 1 yd (90cm)

Ribbon tape ¾ in (1.8cm) wide

for child 39½, 43½ (100, 110cm) tall: 20 in (50cm); 47¼, 51¼ in (120, 130cm) tall:
  24 in (60cm); 55 in (140cm) tall: 28 in (70cm)

Invisible zipper: for 39½, 43½, 47¼ in (100, 110, 120cm) tall: 16 in (40cm) x 1;
  51¼, 55 in (140cm) tall: 20 in (50cm) x 1

Hook and eye x 1 set

#25 embroidery thread as required

INSTRUCTIONS
Preparation: Apply fusible tape at zipper position. *M stitch center back edges of back
  and back yoke, upper edge of front and lower edge of front yoke pieces.

1 Attach ribbon tape to front yoke (see p43)
2 Create gathers at upper edge of dress front and attach ribbon tape (see p43)
3 Create gathers at upper edge of back and attach back yoke
4 Sew center back seam to endpoint of zipper and insert invisible zipper (see p62)
5 Finish back neckline using bias tape (see p18, 20)
6 Sew shoulders (see p18). M stitch through both layers of seam allowance
7 Place front over front yoke pieces and sew (see p43)
8 Sew sides (see p21). M stitch through both layers of seam allowance
9 Create smocking on lower part of sleeve and draw to 4 in (10cm) (see p70, p68)
10 Join upper and lower parts of sleeves. M stitch through both layers of seam allowance
11 Sew undersides of sleeves. M stitch through both layers of seam allowance
12 Double-fold sleeve openings and sew (see p40)
13 Attach sleeves (see p55). M stitch through both layers of
   seam allowance
14 Double-fold hem and sew (see p40)
15 Attach hook and eye (see p64)

  ＊M = use a zigzag stitch to neaten seam allowance

Cutting layout

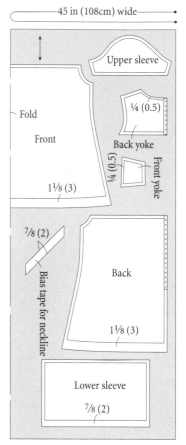

＊ Seam allowances are ⅜ in (1cm) unless otherwise indicated

Shaded area indicates fusible interfacing

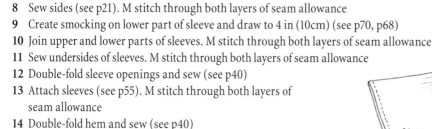

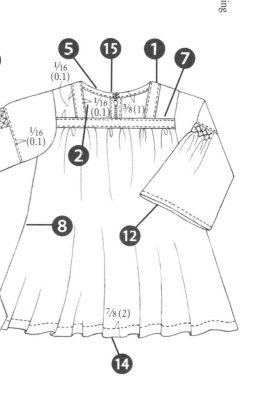

[Basic Pattern 4]

page 28

Full-size pattern piece side C

MATERIALS

[Materials required are the same for all 5 sizes unless otherwise indicated]

FABRIC

Sweatshirt fabric 38 in (96cm) wide (may be sold in a "tube" 19 in [48cm])

for child 39½ in (100cm) tall: ⅞ yd (80cm); 43½ in (110cm) tall: 1⅛ yd (1m);
   47¼ in (120cm) tall: 1¼ yd (1m 10cm); 51¼ in (130cm) tall: 1⅓ yd (1m 20cm);
   55 in (140cm) tall: 1½ yd (1m 30cm)

Elastic ¼–⅜ in (8mm) wide: for child 39½ in (100cm) tall: 37 in (94cm);
   43½ in (110cm) tall: 39 in (98cm); 47¼ in (120cm) tall: 40 in (102cm);
   51¼ in (130cm) tall: 42 in (106cm); 55 in (140cm) tall: 44 in (110cm)
   (including seam allowance)

Tape: ⅜ x 20 in (1 x 50cm) wide

INSTRUCTIONS:

1 Sew crotch for both front and back of pants, leaving seam allowance at back to
   create casing (see p58). *M stitch through both layers of seam allowance
2 Sew sides (see p58). M stitch through both layers of seam allowance
3 Sew inside leg seams (see p58). M stitch through both layers of seam allowance
4 Single-fold waist and sew two rows of zigzag stitch
5 Single-fold hems and finish with zigzag stitch
6 Insert two lengths of elastic through waist casings (see p58)
7 Tie tape in a bow and attach at center front

   ∗ As this design uses sweatshirt material, it can be finished off using single folds
     for steps 4 and 5 where usually double folds would be used
   ∗ M = use a zigzag stitch to neaten seam allowance

Cutting layout

38 in (96cm) wide

[19 in (48cm) tubing]

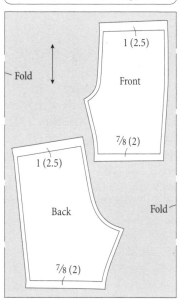

∗ Seam allowances are ⅜ in (1cm) unless otherwise indicated

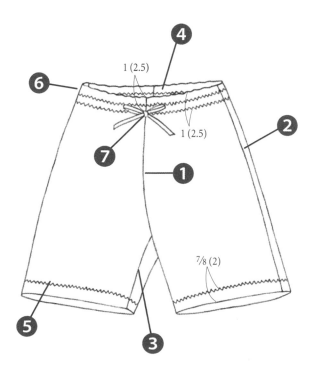

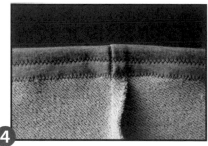

Make a single fold around waist and sew using two rows of zigzag stitch. Insert two lengths of elastic through opening

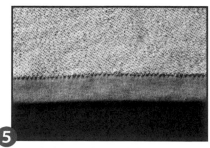

For the hems, make a single fold and sew using zigzag stitch

[Applied Pattern 4]

page 29

Full-size pattern piece side C

MATERIALS

【Materials required are the same for all 5 sizes unless otherwise indicated】

FABRIC

Liberty print 45 in (110cm) wide

for child 39½ in (100cm) tall: 1½ yd (1m 40cm); 43½ in (110cm) tall: 1¾ yd (1m 60cm); 47¼ in (120cm) tall: 2 yd (1m 80cm); 51¼ in (130cm) tall: 2⅛ yd (2m); 55 in (140cm) tall: 2½ yd (2m 30cm)

Fusible interfacing 36 in (90cm) wide

for 39½ in (100cm) tall: 20 in (50cm); 43½, 47¼, 51¼ in (110, 120, 130cm) tall: 24 in (60cm); 55 in (140cm) tall: 28 in (70cm)

Fusible tape ⅝ in (1.5cm) wide

for 39½, 43½, 47¼ in (100, 110, 120cm) tall: 12 in (30cm); 51¼, 55 in (130, 140cm) tall: 16 in (40cm)

Elastic ¼–⅜ in (8mm): for child 39½ in (100cm) tall: 20 in (50cm); 43½ in (110cm) tall: 21 in (52cm); 47¼ in (120cm) tall: 22 in (54cm); 51¼ in (130cm) tall: 22 in (56cm); 55 in (140cm) tall: 23 in (58cm) (including seam allowance)

Buttons: ⅝ in (1.5cm) diameter x 2

INSTRUCTIONS

Preparation: Apply fusible tape to front pocket openings and fusible interfacing to outer piece of bib and outer shoulder straps. *M stitch sides of front and back

1   Create back pocket and attach to back right of pants
2   Create shoulder straps (see p80). Attach strap carrier to left shoulder strap (see p60)
3   Sew front crotch and create tucks (see p60). M stitch through both layers of seam allowance
4   Sew back crotch. Attach fabric loops (see p42). Cut to 1⅞ in [4.5cm] long). Double-fold waist, insert elastic and sew to secure (see p60).
5   Sandwich straps in between bib pieces and sew. Sew bib to pants front (see p60)
6   Sew sides, leaving pocket openings open. Finish off bib (see p61)
7   Create side pockets (see p61)
8   Sew inner leg seams. M stitch through both layers of seam allowance
9   Double-fold hems and sew (see p40)
10 Attach buttons to shoulder straps (see p39)

　　＊M = use a zigzag stitch to neaten seam allowance

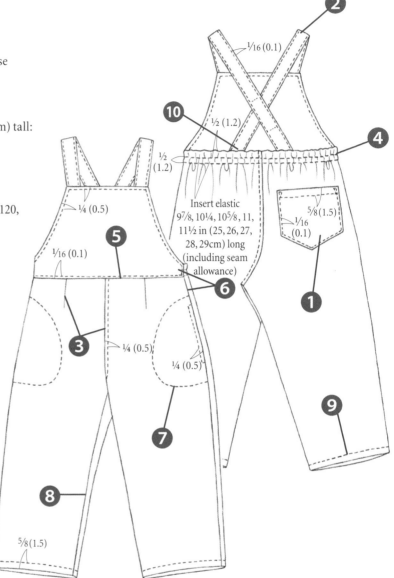

Cutting layout

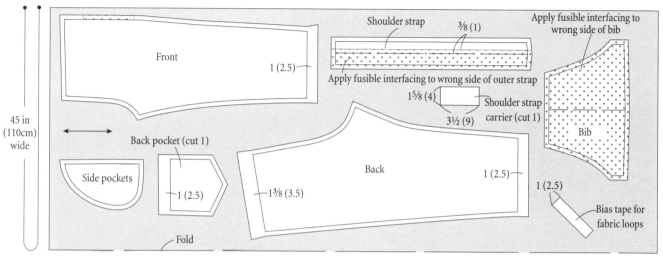

45 in (110cm) wide

Front — 1 (2.5)

Side pockets

Back pocket (cut 1) — 1 (2.5)

Fold

Back — 1 (2.5)

1⅜ (3.5)

Shoulder strap — ⅜ (1)

Apply fusible interfacing to wrong side of outer strap

1⅝ (4) — 3½ (9) — **Shoulder strap carrier (cut 1)**

Apply fusible interfacing to wrong side of bib

Bib

1 (2.5)

Bias tape for fabric loops

＊Seam allowances are ⅜ in (1cm) unless otherwise indicated

Shaded area indicates fusible interfacing

1 When sewing a patch pocket, sew opening edge, then iron heat-fusible double-sided tape around three remaining edges and attach in position. This works in place of basting

[Basic Pattern 5]
page 30

MATERIALS
[Materials required are the same for all 5 sizes unless otherwise indicated]

FABRIC
Cotton check 45 in (110cm) wide
for child 39½ in (100cm) tall: 1⅛ yd (1m);
    43½ in (110cm) tall: 1¼ yd (1m 10cm);
    47¼ in (120cm) tall: 1⅓ yd (1m 20cm);
    51¼ in (130cm) tall: 1½ yd (1m 30cm);
    55 in (140cm) tall: 1½ yd (1m 40cm)
Shirring elastic—1 reel

INSTRUCTIONS
Preparation: *M stitch along upper edge of dress and along sides

1 Sew side seams. Press seams open
2 Create a single fold along upper edge of dress using iron (see p41)
3 Create shoulder ties and attach to dress
4 Create shirring (see p59)
5 Double-fold hem and sew (see p40)

    *M = use a zigzag stitch to neaten seam allowance

Drafting

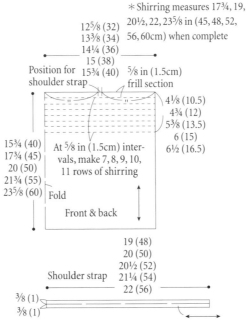

* Shirring measures 17¾, 19, 20½, 22, 23⅝ in (45, 48, 52, 56, 60cm) when complete

12⅝ (32)
13⅜ (34)
14¼ (36)
15 (38)
15¾ (40)

Position for shoulder strap

⅝ in (1.5cm) frill section

4⅛ (10.5)
4¾ (12)
5⅜ (13.5)
6 (15)
6½ (16.5)

15¾ (40)
17¾ (45)
20 (50)
21¾ (55)
23⅝ (60)

At ⅝ in (1.5cm) intervals, make 7, 8, 9, 10, 11 rows of shirring

Fold
Front & back

19 (48)
20 (50)
20½ (52)
21¼ (54)
22 (56)

Shoulder strap

⅜ (1)
⅜ (1)

* Five measurements given are for sizes 39½, 43½, 47¼, 51¼, 55 in (100, 110, 120, 130, 140cm) tall

Cutting layout

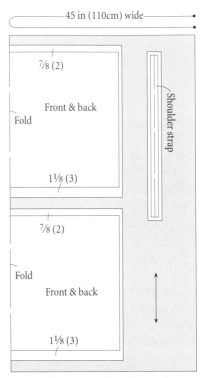

45 in (110cm) wide

⅞ (2)
Front & back
Fold
1⅛ (3)

Shoulder strap

⅞ (2)
Fold
Front & back
1⅛ (3)

* Seam allowances are ⅜ in (1cm) unless otherwise indicated

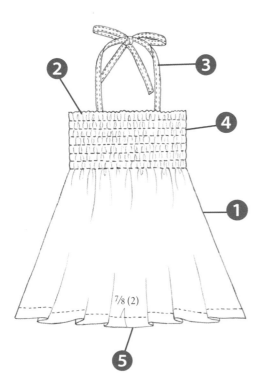

7/8 (2)

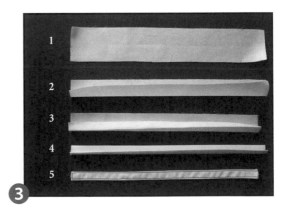

How to create shoulder ties

1 The shoulder tie as cut out
2 Fold so wrong sides meet
3 Open out fold from step 2 and fold ⅜ in (1cm) from each edge into the center
4 The tie folded in half with edges meeting in the center
5 Sew 1/16 in (0.1cm) around edge

[Applied Pattern 5]
page **31**

MATERIALS
【Materials required are the same for all 5 sizes
unless otherwise indicated】

FABRIC
Cotton print, blue, 45 in (110cm) wide
for child 39½ in (100cm) tall: 1 yd (90cm);
    43½ in (110cm) tall: 1⅛ yd (1m);
    47¼ in (120cm) tall: 1¼ yd (1m 10cm);
    51¼ in (130cm) tall: 1½ yd (1m 30cm);
    55 in (140cm) tall: 1½ yd (1m 40cm)
Cotton print, white, 45 in (110cm) wide
39½ in (100cm) tall: ¾ yd (70cm);
    43½ in (110cm) tall:
    ⅞ yd (80cm); 47¼ in (120cm) tall:
    1⅛ yd (1m); 51¼ in (130cm) tall:
    1¼ yd (1m 10cm); 55 in (140cm) tall:
    1⅓ yd (1m 20cm)
Shirring elastic—1 reel

INSTRUCTIONS
Preparation: *M stitch along upper edge of front and
    back for section 1 and along sides

1 Sew front and back of section 1 together at sides and
    open out seam
2 Sew fronts and backs of sections 2, 3 and 4 together
    at sides. M stitch through both layers of seam
    allowance
3 Sew section 1 to section 2. Sew section 2 to section 3.
    M stitch through both layers of seam allowance
4 Create gathers along upper edge of section 4 and sew
    to section 3. M stitch through both layers of seam
    allowance (see p44)
5 Single-fold upper edge of section 1 (see p41)
6 Create shoulder ties (see p80) and attach to dress
7 Create shirring (see p59)
8 Double-fold hem and sew (see p40)
    *M = use a zigzag stitch to neaten seam allowance

Cutting layout (for cotton print/
blue fabric)

Cutting layout (for cotton print/
white fabric)

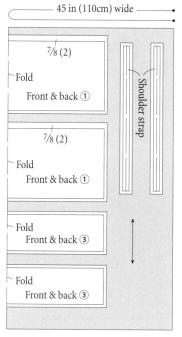

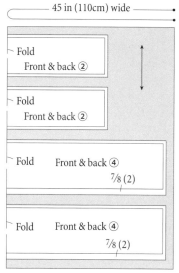

* For sizes 47¼, 51¼, 55 in (120, 130,
140cm), cut 3 pieces of pattern piece 4

* Seam allowances are ⅜ in (1cm)
unless otherwise indicated

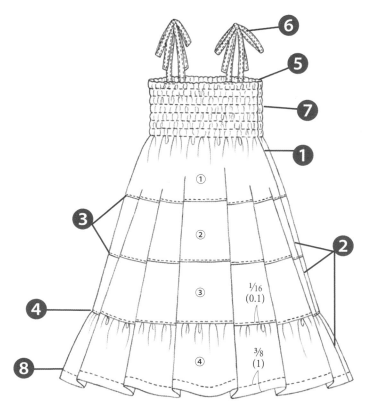

Drafting

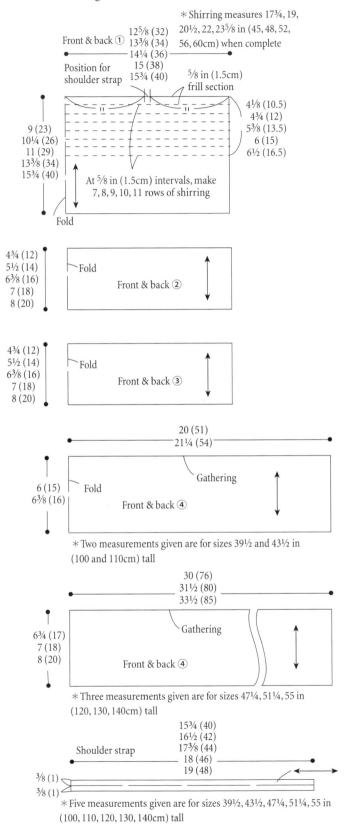

Front & back ①

12⅝ (32)
13⅜ (34)
14¼ (36)
15 (38)
15¾ (40)

* Shirring measures 17¾, 19, 20½, 22, 23⅝ in (45, 48, 52, 56, 60cm) when complete

Position for shoulder strap

⅝ in (1.5cm) frill section

4⅛ (10.5)
4¾ (12)
5⅜ (13.5)
6 (15)
6½ (16.5)

9 (23)
10¼ (26)
11 (29)
13⅜ (34)
15¾ (40)

At ⅝ in (1.5cm) intervals, make 7, 8, 9, 10, 11 rows of shirring

Fold

4¾ (12)
5½ (14)
6⅜ (16)
7 (18)
8 (20)

Fold

Front & back ②

4¾ (12)
5½ (14)
6⅜ (16)
7 (18)
8 (20)

Fold

Front & back ③

20 (51)
21¼ (54)

6 (15)
6⅜ (16)

Fold

Gathering

Front & back ④

* Two measurements given are for sizes 39½ and 43½ in (100 and 110cm) tall

30 (76)
31½ (80)
33½ (85)

6¾ (17)
7 (18)
8 (20)

Gathering

Front & back ④

* Three measurements given are for sizes 47¼, 51¼, 55 in (120, 130, 140cm) tall

Shoulder strap

15¾ (40)
16½ (42)
17⅜ (44)
18 (46)
19 (48)

⅜ (1)
⅜ (1)

* Five measurements given are for sizes 39½, 43½, 47¼, 51¼, 55 in (100, 110, 120, 130, 140cm) tall

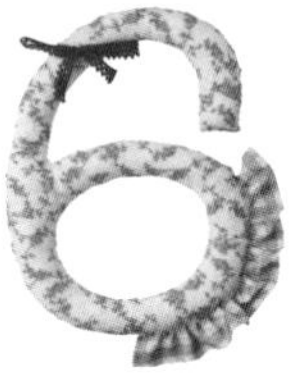

[Basic Pattern 6]

page 32

Full-size pattern piece side D

Cutting layout (for plain cotton)

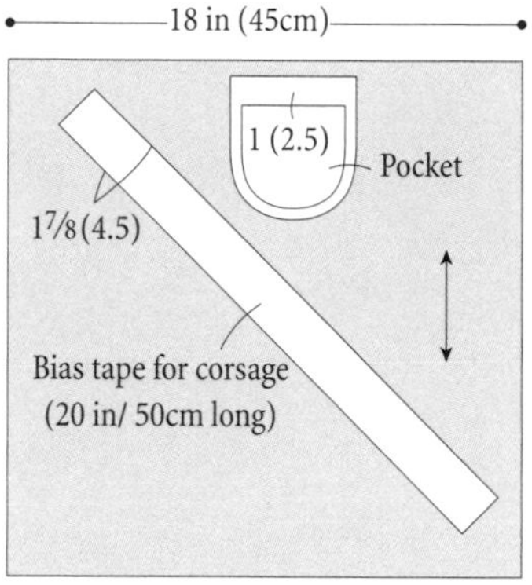
18 in (45cm)
1 (2.5)
Pocket
1⅞ (4.5)
Bias tape for corsage
(20 in/ 50cm long)

Cutting layout (for liberty print)

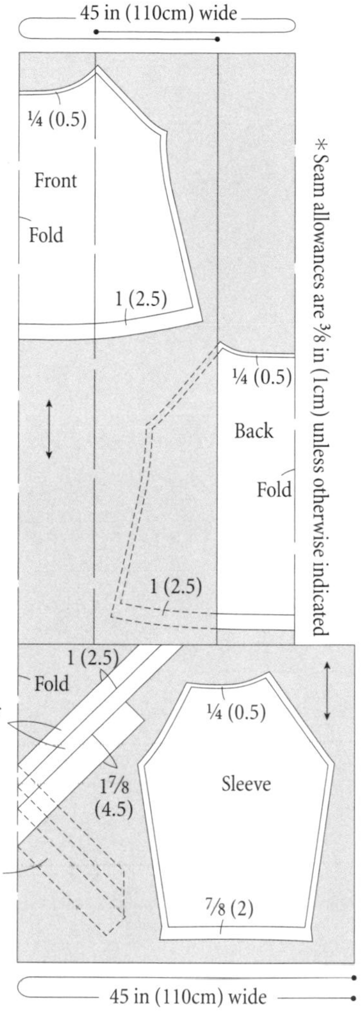
45 in (110cm) wide
¼ (0.5)
Front
Fold
1 (2.5)
¼ (0.5)
Back
Fold
1 (2.5)
*Seam allowances are ⅜ in (1cm) unless otherwise indicated
1 (2.5)
Fold
Bias tape for
neckline
1⅞
(4.5)
¼ (0.5)
Sleeve
Bias tape for
corsage (20 in/
50cm long)
⅞ (2)
45 in (110cm) wide

MATERIALS

[Materials required are the same for all 5 sizes unless otherwise indicated]

FABRIC

Liberty print 45 in (110cm) wide

for child 39½ in (100cm) tall: 1⅝ yd (1m 50cm);
43½ in (110cm) tall: 1⅞ yd (1m 70cm);
47¼ in (120cm) tall: 2⅛ yd (1m 90cm);
51¼ in (130cm) tall: 2⅛ yd (2m);
55 in (140cm) tall: 2⅜ yd (2m 20cm)

Plain fabric—18 x 18 in (45 x 45cm)

Elastic ¼ or ⅜ inches (8mm) for child 39½ in (100cm) tall: 28 in (70cm); 43½ in (110cm) tall: 29 in (74cm); 47¼ in (120cm) tall: 31 in (78cm); 51¼ in (130cm) tall: 33 in (82cm); 55 in (140cm) tall: 34 in (86cm) (including seam allowance)

INSTRUCTIONS

1 Create pocket and attach to blouse (see p70)
2 Attach front and back pieces to sleeves (see p65).
*M stitch through both layers of seam allowance
3 Bind neckline using bias tape (see p65)
4 Sew underside of sleeves and side seams in a continuous seam (see p65). M stitch through both layers of seam allowance
5 Double-fold sleeve openings and sew (see p40)
6 Double-fold hem and sew (see p40)
7 Insert elastic through casings at neck and sleeve openings (see p53)

*M = use a zigzag stitch to neaten seam allowance

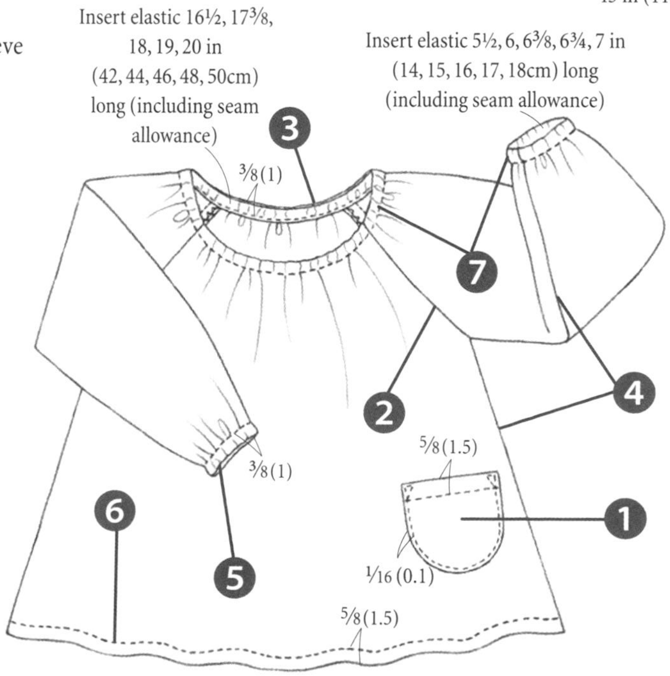
Insert elastic 16½, 17⅜,
18, 19, 20 in
(42, 44, 46, 48, 50cm)
long (including seam
allowance)
Insert elastic 5½, 6, 6⅜, 6¾, 7 in
(14, 15, 16, 17, 18cm) long
(including seam allowance)
3
⅜(1)
7
2
4
⅝(1.5)
⅜(1)
6
1
5
1⁄16 (0.1)
⅝(1.5)

Corsage

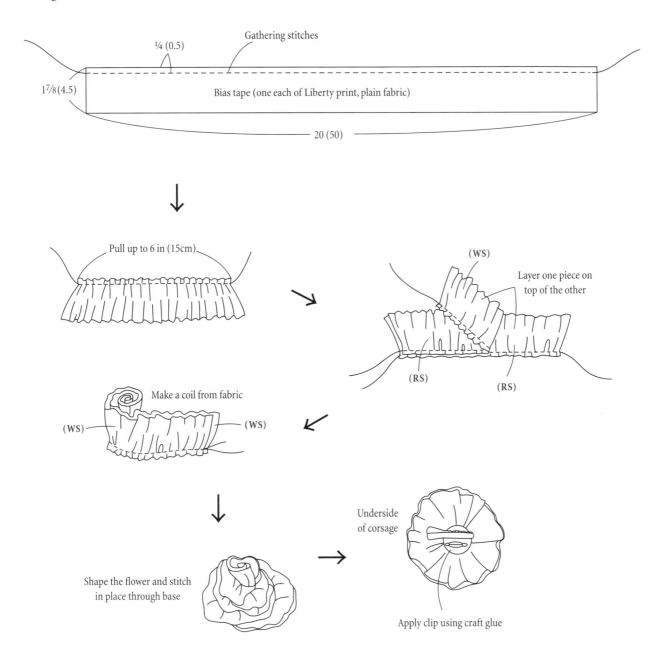

Gathering stitches

¼ (0.5)

1⅞ (4.5)

Bias tape (one each of Liberty print, plain fabric)

20 (50)

Pull up to 6 in (15cm)

(WS)

Layer one piece on top of the other

(RS)   (RS)

Make a coil from fabric

(WS)   (WS)

Shape the flower and stitch in place through base

Underside of corsage

Apply clip using craft glue

[Applied Pattern 6 a]

page 33

Full-size pattern piece side D

MATERIALS

[Materials required are the same for all 5 sizes unless otherwise indicated]

FABRIC

Liberty print 45 in (110cm) wide

for child 39½ in (100cm) tall: 1½ yd (1m 40cm);

43½ in (110cm) tall: 1¾ yd (1m 60cm);

47¼ in (120cm) tall: 2 yd (1m 80cm); 51¼ in (130cm) tall:

2⅛ yd (1m 90cm); 55 in (140cm) tall: 2¼ yd (2m 10cm)

Plain fabric: 22 x 20 in (55 x 50cm)

Elastic ¼–⅜ inch (8mm) for child 39½ in (100cm) tall:

16½ in (42cm); 43½ in (110cm) tall: 17⅜ in (44cm);

47¼ in (120cm) tall: 18⅛ in (46cm); 51¼ in (130cm)

19 in (48cm); 55 in (140cm) tall 20 in (50cm)

INSTRUCTIONS

1 Create pocket and attach to smock (see p70)
2 Double-fold sleeve opening and sew (see p40)
3 Attach sleeves to smock front and back.
   *M stitch through both layers of seam allowance
4 Bind neckline using bias tape (see p65 *apply bias tape on right side of fabric). Insert elastic through casing (see p53)
5 Sew sides (see p21). M stitch through both layers of seam allowance
6 Double-fold hem and sew (see p40)
7 Create ribbon ⅜ in (1cm) wide from bias tape (see p42) and attach over stitching on left side

   * M = use a zigzag stitch to neaten seam allowance

Cutting layout (for plain cotton)

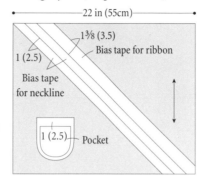

Cutting layout (for liberty print)

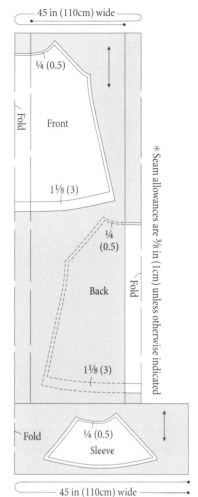

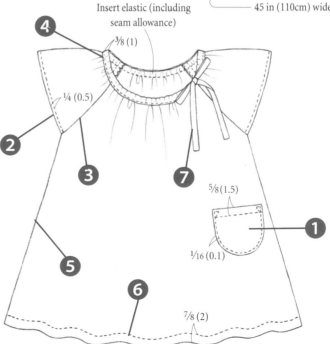

2 **3** Double-fold sleeve opening and sew
Sew sleeve and body pieces together
and press seams towards body

[Applied Pattern 6 b]

page 33

Full-size pattern piece side D

MATERIALS

[Materials required are the same for all 5 sizes unless otherwise indicated]

FABRIC

Plain cotton 45 in (110cm) wide

for child 39½ in (100cm) tall: 1⅓ yd (1m 20cm);

    43½ in (110cm) tall: 1½ yd (1m 30cm);

    47¼ in (120cm) tall: 1½ yd (1m 40cm);

    51¼ in (130cm) tall: 1⅝ yd (1m 50cm);

    55 in (140cm) tall: 1¾ yd (1m 60cm)

Tulle 74 in (188cm) wide

    for child 39½ in (100cm), 47¼ in (120cm) tall:

    ⅝ yd (60cm); 51¼, 55 in (130, 140cm): ¾ yd (70cm)

INSTRUCTIONS

1 Sew side seams of base dress (see p21).
   *M stitch through both layers of seam allowance

2 Sew side seams of tulle. Open out seams (see p43)

3 Double-fold hem of base dress and sew (see p40)

4 Layer tulle over base dress and bind armholes in bias tape (see p19, 43)

5 Gather neckline at front and back and bind using bias tape (see p19, 43)

   ✳ M = use a zigzag stitch to neaten seam allowance

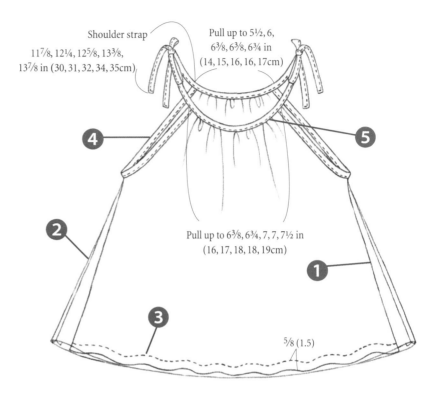

Shoulder strap
11⅞, 12¼, 12⅝, 13⅜, 13⅞ in (30, 31, 32, 34, 35cm)

Pull up to 5½, 6, 6⅜, 6⅜, 6¾ in (14, 15, 16, 16, 17cm)

Pull up to 6⅜, 6¾, 7, 7, 7½ in (16, 17, 18, 18, 19cm)

⅝ (1.5)

Cut tulle without adding seam allowances for side seams or hem

Cutting layout (for plain cotton)

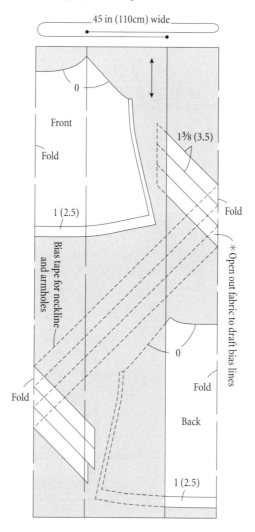

45 in (110cm) wide

0

Front

Fold

1 (2.5)

1³⁄₈ (3.5)

Fold

Bias tape for neckline and armholes

∗Open out fabric to draft bias lines

0

Fold

Back

Fold

1 (2.5)

Cutting layout (tulle)

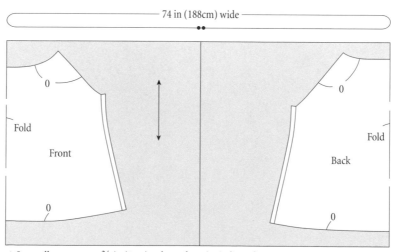

74 in (188cm) wide

0

Fold

Front

0

0

Fold

Back

0

∗ Seam allowances are ³⁄₈ in (1cm) unless otherwise indicated

[Basic Pattern 7]
page 34
Full-size pattern piece side A

MATERIALS
[Materials required are the same for all 5 sizes
unless otherwise indicated]

FABRIC
Cotton print 45 in (110cm) wide
for child 100 cm tall: 1 yd (90cm); 43½ in (110cm) tall:
1⅛ yd (1m); 47¼ in (120cm) tall: 1¼ yd (1m 10cm);
51¼ in (130cm) tall: 1⅓ yd (1m 20cm);
55 in (140cm) tall: 1½ yd (1m 30cm)
Fusible interfacing 36 in (90cm) wide
for child 39½ in (100cm) tall: 16 in (40cm);
43½, 47¼, 51¼, 55 in (110, 120, 130, 140cm) tall:
20 in (50cm)
Flower-shaped buttons: ½ in (1.2cm) diameter x 5

INSTRUCTIONS
Preparation: Apply fusible interfacing to front and back
armhole facings, front facing and collar. *M stitch outer
edge of armhole facings and front facing.
1   Create frills and attach to front of dress
2   Sew shoulders (see p18). M stitch through both layers of
seam allowance
3   Create collar (see p49)
4   Match right sides of dress and facings and sew from
collar endpoint along front edges (see p50)
5   Attach collar. Finish off neckline using facings and bias
tape (see p50)
6   Complete armholes using facings (see p56)
7   Sew from armhole facings to side seams in a continuous
seam. M stitch through both layers of seam allowance.
Sew around armholes (see p57)
8   Double-fold hem and sew (see p40)
9   Create buttonholes and attach buttons (see p39)
    *M = use a zigzag stitch to neaten seam allowance

1 Once the dress front is cut out, leave the pattern on the fabric and use a roulette wheel to mark frill positions

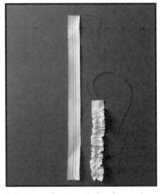

2 Create gathering stitches by sewing from one end of the frill around and back along stitching lines. Draw threads up

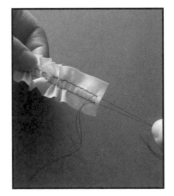

2' Hold frill in your left hand and pull both threads at the same time, distributing gathers evenly

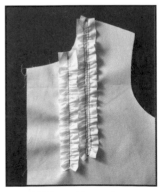

3 Sew frills in position on dress, stitching down center of frill. Remove gathering threads

Cutting layout

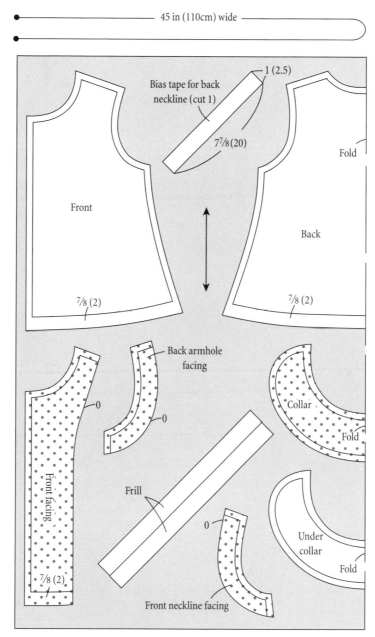

45 in (110cm) wide

Bias tape for back neckline (cut 1)

1 (2.5)

7⅞ (20)

Front

Fold

Back

⅞ (2)

⅞ (2)

Back armhole facing

0

0

Collar

Fold

Front facing

Frill

0

Under collar

Fold

⅞ (2)

Front neckline facing

✳ Seam allowances are ⅜ in (1cm) unless otherwise indicated

▦ Shaded area indicates fusible interfacing

[Applied Pattern 7]

page 35

Full-size pattern piece side A

MATERIALS

【Materials required are the same for all 5 sizes unless otherwise indicated】

FABRIC

Linen 45 in (114cm) wide

for child 39½ in (100cm) tall: 1¼ yd (1m 10cm); 43½ in (110cm) tall:
1⅓ yd (1m 20cm); 47¼ in (120cm) tall: 1½ yd (1m 30cm); 51¼ in (130cm) tall:
1⅞ yd (1m 70cm); 55 in (140cm) tall: 2 yd (1m 80cm)

Fusible interfacing 36 in (90cm) wide

for child 39½, 43½, 47¼ in (100, 110, 120cm) tall: 20 in (50cm);
51¼, 55 in (130, 140cm) tall: 24 in (60cm)

Self-cover button ⅝ in (1.5cm) diameter x 4

#25 embroidery thread as required

INSTRUCTIONS

Preparation: Apply fusible interfacing to front facing, front and back armhole facings and collar.
*M stitch around outer edges of armhole facings and front facing. Embroider collar and pocket (see p95)

1 Create pocket and attach to dress (see p15)

2 Sew center front seam to end of opening (see p66). M stitch through both layers of seam allowance

3 Attach facing to finish front opening (see p66)

4 Sew shoulders (see p18). M stitch through both layers of seam allowance

5 Create collar. Finish off neckline by attaching facing to front neckline and binding back neckline using bias tape (see p67)

6 Attach armhole facings (see p56)

7 Sew sides. M stitch through both layers of seam allowance. Sew around armholes (see p57)

8 Double-fold hem and sew (see p40)

9 Create buttonholes and attach buttons (see p39)

  *M = use a zigzag stitch to neaten seam allowance

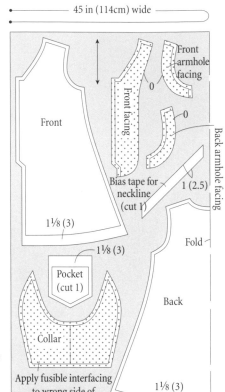

Cutting layout

45 in (114cm) wide

Front

Front facing

Front armhole facing

0

0

Bias tape for neckline (cut 1)

1 (2.5)

Back armhole facing

1⅛ (3)

1⅛ (3)

Pocket (cut 1)

Fold

Back

Collar

Apply fusible interfacing to wrong side of outer collar only

1⅛ (3)

✳ Seam allowances are ⅜ in (1cm) unless otherwise indicated

Shaded area indicates fusible interfacing

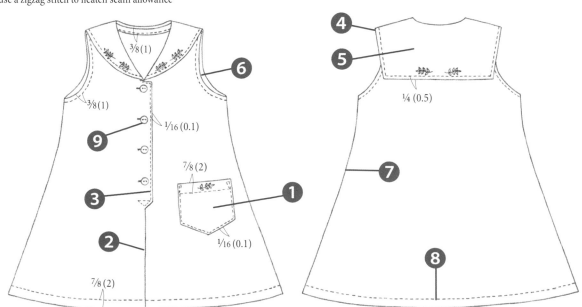

⅜ (1)

⅜ (1)

1/16 (0.1)

⅞ (2)

1/16 (0.1)

⅞ (2)

¼ (0.5)

[Basic Pattern 8]

page 36

Full-size pattern piece side D

MATERIALS

【Materials required are the same for all 5 sizes unless otherwise indicated】

FABRIC

Double gauze 42 in (106cm) wide

for child 39½ in (100cm) tall: 1⅛ yd (1m); 43½ in (110cm) tall:
   1¼ yd (1m 10cm); 47¼ in (120cm) tall: 1⅓ yd (1m 20cm);
   51¼ in (130cm) tall: 1⅜ yd (1m 30cm); 55 in (140cm) tall:
   1½ yd (1m 40cm)

Self-cover button 1⅛ in (2.8cm) diameter x 1

Ric-rac: for 39½ in (100cm) tall: 2¼ yd (2m 10cm);
   43½ in (110cm) tall: 2⅜ yd (2m 20cm); 47¼ in (120cm) tall:
   2⅜ yd (2m 20cm); 51¼ in (130cm) tall: 2⅝ yd (2m 40cm);
   55 in (140cm) tall: 2¾ yd (2m 50cm)

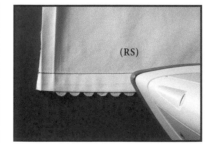

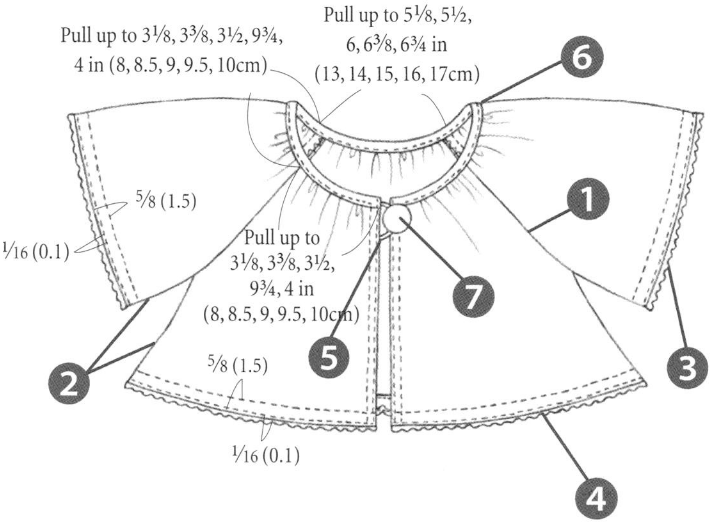

Pull up to 3⅛, 3⅜, 3½, 9¾, 4 in (8, 8.5, 9, 9.5, 10cm)

Pull up to 5⅛, 5½, 6, 6⅜, 6¾ in (13, 14, 15, 16, 17cm)

⅝ (1.5)

1/16 (0.1)

Pull up to 3⅛, 3⅜, 3½, 9¾, 4 in (8, 8.5, 9, 9.5, 10cm)

⅝ (1.5)

1/16 (0.1)

INSTRUCTIONS

1 Sew front and back pieces to sleeves (see p65).
   *M stitch through both layers of seam allowance

2 Sew underside of sleeves and sides in a continuous seam.
   M stitch through both layers of seam allowance

3 Double-fold sleeve openings (see p40) and attach ric-rac

4 Double-fold hem and sew (see p40) and attach ric-rac

5 Create fabric loop (see p42. Cut to 2¾ in [7cm] long) and attach to front
   edge. Double-fold front edge and sew

6 Create gathers around neckline, bind neckline using bias tape (see p18, 19)

7 Create self-cover button and attach

   * M = use a zigzag stitch to neaten seam allowance

Attaching the ric-rac

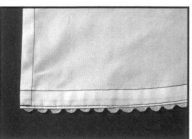

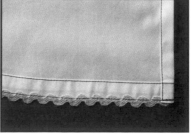

1 Attach ¼ in (0.5cm) wide
heat-fusible double-sided tape
to ric-rac

2 Position ric-rac under fabric
edge so that the edge/scallop
shows on right side

(RS)

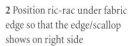

3 Sew 1/16 in (0.1cm) from edge
of fabric

4 Finished edge shown from
wrong side

Cutting layout

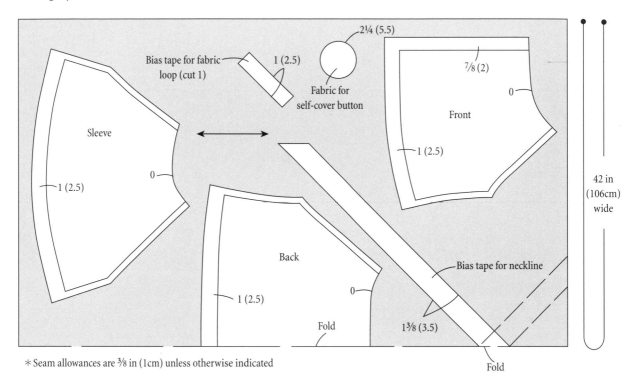

Bias tape for fabric loop (cut 1)
1 (2.5)

2¼ (5.5)
Fabric for self-cover button

Sleeve
1 (2.5)
0

⅞ (2)
0
Front
1 (2.5)

Back
1 (2.5)
0

Bias tape for neckline

1⅜ (3.5)

Fold

Fold

42 in (106cm) wide

＊Seam allowances are ⅜ in (1cm) unless otherwise indicated

7 Full-size embroidery diagrams for applied pattern

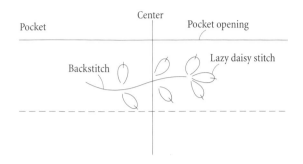

Pocket · Center · Pocket opening

Backstitch · Lazy daisy stitch

How to transfer embroidery diagrams

Using sewing or embroidery transfer paper is one of a few ways to do this. Lay down your transfer paper, waxy/colored side up. Place your fabric down over it, right side up. Place your pattern over the fabric. Using a dried ballpoint or a stylus, go over the pattern markings, pressing hard while taking care not to tear the pattern. The image will be transferred to the wrong side of the fabric

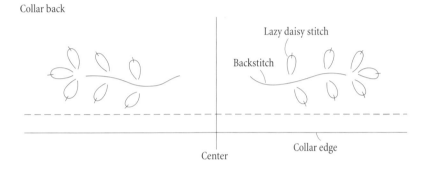

Collar back

Lazy daisy stitch

Backstitch

Collar edge

Center

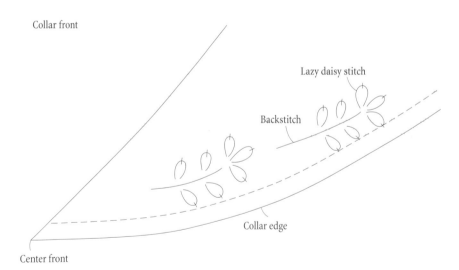

Collar front

Lazy daisy stitch

Backstitch

Collar edge

Center front

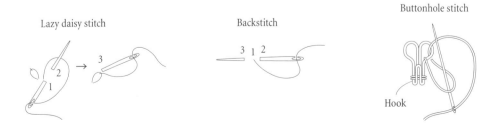

Lazy daisy stitch

Backstitch

Buttonhole stitch

Hook

Published in 2014 by Tuttle Publishing, an imprint of Periplus Editions (HK) Ltd.

www.tuttlepublishing.com

ISBN 978-4-8053-1327-5

TANOSHIKU MANABERU ONNA NO KO NO TAME NO FUKUZUKURI NO KISO
by Yoshiko TSUKIORI
© 2011 Yoshiko TSUKIORI
English translation rights arranged with
EDUCATIONAL FOUNDATION BUNKA GAKUEN BUNKA PUBLISHING BUREAU
through Japan UNI Agency, Inc. Tokyo
Translated from Japanese by Leeyong Soo
All rights reserved.

Original Japanese edition
Publisher: Sunao Onuma
Cover and layout by Mihoko Amano
Photography by Yasuo Nagumo
Styling by Tomoe Ito
Hair and make-up by Noriko Suzuki
Modelling by Alice Okuma, Reika Hargrave
Tracing by Toshio Usui
How-to diagrams/drawings created by Kumiko Kurokawa
Pattern adaptation by Akiko Kobayashi
Pattern tracing by Act A2
Proofreading by Masako Mukai
Editing by Tomoe Horie and Norie Hirai (Bunka Publishing Bureau)

Distributed by

North America, Latin America & Europe
Tuttle Publishing, 364 Innovation Drive,
North Clarendon, VT 05759-9436 U.S.A.
Tel: 1 (802) 773-8930; Fax: 1 (802) 773-6993
info@tuttlepublishing.com; www.tuttlepublishing.com

Japan
Tuttle Publishing, Yaekari Building, 3rd Floor, 5-4-12 Osaki,
Shinagawa-ku, Tokyo 141 0032
Tel: (81) 3 5437-0171; Fax: (81) 3 5437-0755
sales@tuttle.co.jp; www.tuttle.co.jp

Asia Pacific
Berkeley Books Pte. Ltd.
61 Tai Seng Avenue #02-12, Singapore 534167
Tel: (65) 6280-1330; Fax: (65) 6280-6290
inquiries@periplus.com.sg; www.periplus.com

Printed in Malaysia   1411TW
17 16 15 14   6 5 4 3 2 1

The Tuttle Story
"Books to Span the East and West"

Many people are surprised to learn that the world's largest publisher of books on Asia had its humble beginnings in the tiny American state of Vermont. The company's founder, Charles E. Tuttle, belonged to a New England family steeped in publishing.

Tuttle's father was a noted antiquarian dealer in Rutland, Vermont. Young Charles honed his knowledge of the trade working in the family bookstore, and later in the rare books section of Columbia University Library. His passion for beautiful books—old and new—never wavered throughout his long career as a bookseller and publisher.

After graduating from Harvard, Tuttle enlisted in the military and in 1945 was sent to Tokyo to work on General Douglas MacArthur's staff. He was tasked with helping to revive the Japanese publishing industry, which had been utterly devastated by the war. When his tour of duty was completed, he left the military, married a talented and beautiful singer, Reiko Chiba, and in 1948 began several successful business ventures.

To his astonishment, Tuttle discovered that postwar Tokyo was actually a book-lover's paradise. He befriended dealers in the Kanda district and began supplying rare Japanese editions to American libraries. He also imported American books to sell to the thousands of GIs stationed in Japan. By 1949, Tuttle's business was thriving, and he opened Tokyo's very first English-language bookstore in the Takashimaya Department Store in Ginza, to great success. Two years later, he began publishing books to fulfill the growing interest of foreigners in all things Asian.

Though a westerner, Tuttle was hugely instrumental in bringing a knowledge of Japan and Asia to a world hungry for information about the East. By the time of his death in 1993, he had published over 6,000 books on Asian culture, history and art—a legacy honored by Emperor Hirohito in 1983 with the "Order of the Sacred Treasure," the highest honor Japan can bestow upon a non-Japanese.

The Tuttle company today maintains an active backlist of some 1,500 titles, many of which have been continuously in print since the 1950s and 1960s—a great testament to Charles Tuttle's skill as a publisher. More than 60 years after its founding, Tuttle Publishing is more active today than at any time in its history, still inspired by Charles Tuttle's core mission—to publish fine books to span the East and West and provide a greater understanding of each.